As You Go

An Honest Look at
the First Followers of Jesus

As You Go

An Honest Look at
the First Followers of Jesus

W. Hulitt Gloer

PEAKE ROAD

Macon, Georgia

ISBN 1-57312-007-3

As You Go
An Honest Look at the First Followers of Jesus

W. Hulitt Gloer

Copyright © 1996
Peake Road

6316 Peake Road
Macon, Georgia 31210-3960
1-800-747-3016

Peake Road
is an imprint of
Smyth & Helwys Publishing, Inc.®

Library of Congress Cataloging-in-Publication Data

Gloer, Hulitt.
    As you go: an honest look at the first followers of Jesus/
W. Hulitt Gloer.
    viii + 120 pp.   6" x 9" (15 x 23 cm.)
    Includes bibliographical references.
    ISBN 1-57312-007-3 (alk. paper)
    1. Apostles—Biography. 2. Bible. N.T.—Biography. I. Title.
    BS2440.G47   1996
    225.9'22—dc20   95-48115
    [B]   CIP

Contents

Preface

A century ago, a Kansas pastor named Charles Sheldon wrote a little book that was destined to become a devotional classic. Since its publication in 1896, *In His Steps* has sold more than 30,000,000 copies. Despite the fact that its setting is vintage turn-of-the-century Americana, it has been translated into more than twenty languages. The publisher's introduction to a 1973 reprint suggests that *In His Steps*

> deserves a place among great religious books not because it represents impeccable literary craftsmanship but because it clings to the idea and the ideal that captured the imagination of millions—[that] the teaching of Jesus Christ is indeed practical and workable if fearlessly put to the test.[1]

That test, according to Sheldon, is simply this: Before every undertaking, ask the question, "What would Jesus do?"

Sheldon's narrative of the revolutionary consequences that ensue ·when the people of a fictional American city set out to apply that test has been called a "novelistic essay on modern Christian discipleship."[2] While it has often been criticized as too simplistic, the continuing popularity of the book is evidence that it continues to strike a chord in the lives of Christians. It sets squarely before us the fundamental question that confronts every generation of believers: What does it mean to be a disciple of Jesus?

Surely there is no more important or pressing question than this for the contemporary Christian. It is, in fact, the inevitable question for all persons who respond to Jesus' call, a call that is the same in all four Gospels and a call that rings through the corridors of time. It is the call to "follow me." Indeed, in their provocative little book *Resident Aliens,* Stanley Hauerwas and William Willimon remind us: "With a simple 'Follow Me,' Jesus invited ordinary people to come out and be part of an adventure, a journey that kept surprising them at every turn in the road."[3] The question is, of course, what is the meaning of this simple statement, "Follow Me?" How are we to understand this adventure? What is the nature of this journey to which Jesus calls us?

In the pages that follow, I tell the story of the first people who answered Jesus' call, the first ordinary women to become a part of this adventure, the first ordinary men to embark on this journey with Jesus. We will meet those men and women who were the first to struggle with what it means to follow Jesus. Together we will examine their lives as the New Testament and early Christian traditions set them before us. From their lives we will seek to discover the characteristics that make for genuine discipleship as we join them, indeed as we follow them on their journey with Jesus.

In one sense, then, the aim of this book is informational. It is to learn what we can about these ordinary people whose lives took on the caste of the extraordinary as a result of their incredible journey. In another sense, however, the aim of this book is ultimately transformational. The stories of the first disciples challenge us to consider the nature of our own response to the call of Jesus as we consider together the characteristics and commitments that marked their lives. Come along then . . . let us join these first disciples on their journey with Jesus in order that we may be more faithful on our own!

Notes

[1]Charles Sheldon, *In His Steps* (Nashville TN: Broadman, 1973).
[2]Ibid.
[3]Stanley Hauerwas and William Willimon, *Resident Aliens* (Nashville: Abingdon, 1989) 49.

Andrew

Biblical Texts
Mark 9:35; 10:41-45; John 1:36-44; 6:5-14; 12:20-22

W e begin our journey with Jesus with a look at the disciple who, according to the Gospel of John, was the first to respond to his call. The early Christians gave this disciple the title *protokletos,* which means "first-called," but we know him as Andrew. He was from the city of Bethsaida, a prosperous village on the northeastern shore of the Sea of Galilee from which he and his brother Simon Peter managed the family fishing business (John 1:44).

From Bethsaida it was an easy walk to Capernaum in one direction and to several significant cities of the Decapolis in the other. These cities of the Decapolis were Gentile cities that had been established by the Greeks for the dissemination of Greek culture in the region. Their influence is evidenced by the fact that two of Jesus' disciples from Bethsaida, Andrew and Philip, bore Greek names. The name Andrew meant "manly."

The Gospel of John gives us the clearest picture of Andrew. In its pages we meet him on three separate occasions, and each time we learn something significant about what it means to be a disciple of Jesus, what it means to journey with him.

Openness to Truth
Reflection Text
John 1:36-41

We first meet Andrew in what seems an unlikely place. He is not in Bethsaida, not even around the Sea of Galilee, but in the region of the Jordan River where John the Baptist was preaching, teaching, and baptizing. In fact, in this first encounter with Andrew we learn that he was originally a disciple of John the Baptist! He must have been one of those Jews who longed for the coming of the promised Messiah and the kingdom he would bring. No doubt this longing had brought him to John, who called the people to repent and prepare themselves for the arrival of the "coming one" and his kingdom.

Clearly, Andrew was concerned about the righteousness that God demanded and expected from people. Perhaps he had become frustrated and disillusioned by the fact that so many citizens of Bethsaida seemed so willing to abandon the ways of their forebears and embrace the ways of the Greeks. In John's preaching, Andrew heard the call to repentance, a call directed to both Jews and Gentiles, and he had responded to that call. Andrew had been baptized by John in the Jordan, and together with his teacher he waited for the arrival of the kingdom of God and the one who would inaugurate it.

Imagine the thrill that Andrew must have felt when one day John pointed to Jesus and said, "Look, here is the lamb of God!" (John 1:36). Hearing his teacher's witness to Jesus, Andrew left John to follow Jesus without hesitation. What does this tell us about Andrew? It tells us that he was open to truth. He had come to John in search of that truth. Now having listened faithfully to his teacher, he was prepared to move on, to take the next step in the search, even if it meant leaving the security of his established relationship with John. Andrew was willing to move *from* where he was *to* where he needed to be. He was willing to move beyond established relationships and routines to new relationships and new ways of doing things. The change would not be easy for Andrew—it never is. Still this is a significant characteristic of genuine discipleship. A disciple is open to truth and prepared to pursue that truth wherever it may lead, whatever it may cost.

Notice the nature of Jesus' call to Andrew. When Jesus saw Andrew and the other disciple following, he asked them what they were seeking. When they answered that they wanted to know where he was staying, Jesus said, "Come and see." This is Jesus' call to anyone who would be his disciples. It is the call to "come and see" (John 1:39)—to come and see a new way of life, a new creation that God is creating in Jesus Christ. In order to be open to this call, we must be open to truth. We must be ready to move *from* where we are *to* where he is calling us to be. Are you prepared to respond to this call? Are you ready to "come and see"? Are you willing to move from where you are in your spiritual life to where Jesus is calling you to be?

Introduces Others to Jesus
Reflection Texts
John 1:40-42; 6:6-8; 12:20-22

We first met Andrew as he discovered the truth that the promised Messiah had come in the person of Jesus of Nazareth. Having discovered that truth, he went immediately to share the truth with others and to bring them to Jesus. In fact, every time we meet Andrew in the Gospel of John he is introducing others to Jesus. In John 1:40-42 we learn that he went immediately to find his brother Simon Peter so that he might share the news of his discovery. Then in John 6 he introduces a little lad to Jesus. Finally, in John 12 we find him introducing a group of Greeks to Jesus. Let us examine two of these incidents more carefully.

In the first incident Andrew seeks out his brother and announces that he has found the Messiah. Then he takes his brother to introduce him to Jesus. It is exciting to see Andrew's concern for those persons who are nearest and dearest to him. Someone has wisely said that those who are looking for something to do for Jesus will find it in their own homes. Indeed, the disciple's mission field begins in her own home, with his own family. True, there is no more difficult place to bear witness for Christ than among those who know us best. It may even be easier to bear witness on the foreign mission field than in our own home or community. Still the call is clear; and when we remember that the gospel is the most important message that anyone, near or far away, can ever hear, how can we keep from sharing it with those we love the most?

Take a few moments right now and think of your own family. Are there persons near you who need to hear the gospel? Are there people in your own family, among your own friends and acquaintances, in your own neighborhood who need to be introduced to Jesus? This is the mission of a disciple.

John 12 tells us of events that occurred in Jerusalem during the last week of Jesus' life. On one occasion some Greeks who had come to Jerusalem to celebrate the Passover came seeking Jesus. They were probably "Godfearers," that is, Gentiles who had been attracted to Judaism and even worshiped regularly in the synagogue but who had not converted to Judaism. Apparently these Greeks had heard about Jesus and wanted to meet and talk with him. They first went to Philip (the other disciple from Bethsaida who, like Andrew, had a Greek name) with their request. Rather than taking them to Jesus, however, Philip went to Andrew with their request. Then together they went to Jesus.

Why do you suppose Philip went to Andrew first? Some scholars have suggested that Andrew may have functioned as a kind of appointment secretary for Jesus. Whether or not this was the case, clearly Andrew had come to be perceived by Philip as one who introduced others to Jesus, and here Andrew introduced these Greeks to Jesus. Andrew's actions reveal a significant insight into his understanding of the nature of the gospel. We know from the book of Acts that the early church experienced a significant struggle with regard to the mission to the Gentiles. The intensity of this struggle is clearly seen when we remember that Andrew's own brother, Simon Peter, was not convinced that Gentiles could become Christians without first becoming Jews until he received a vision from heaven, a vision that did not come until Acts 10!

Andrew had perceived that the gospel was for *all* people—Jew *and* Gentile. He seemed to understand that the good news must be shared with all people. Andrew sought to introduce those persons closest to him and those from far away to Jesus. He was willing to introduce those who were very much like him and those who were very different from him to Jesus. He was always ready to introduce others, any others and all others, to Jesus. This is the mark of a disciple.

Now stop for a moment and consider how God was able to use those persons Andrew brought to Jesus. His brother, Simon Peter, became the leader of the disciple band and one of the greatest leaders of the early church. Jesus was able to use a little lad and his resources of five loaves and two fish to feed more than 5,000 people. And then there were those Greeks. While we do not know for sure the outcome of their encounter with Jesus, possibly some of them believed and then took the good news about Jesus back to their homeland. You see, only God knows the potential of the people we introduce to Jesus.

Edward Kimball was a successful merchant in Boston. One day he met a young shoe salesman. The young man was poor and lonely, with few family members or friends in the city. Kimball shared his faith with that young man and took him to Sunday School. The young man's name was Dwight L. Moody. He went on to have a ministry of such significance that it has been said that he took Europe in one hand and America in the other and brought them together under the banner of the cross. I dare say that Edward Kimball could never have imagined such a thing when he introduced that young man to Jesus.

Andrew introduced others to Jesus. God used Andrew's witness and the persons he introduced to Jesus to accomplish things that Andrew could never in his wildest dreams have imagined. Try to envision what God may be ready to do with those we introduce to Jesus.

Commitment to the Humility of Servanthood
Reflection Texts
Mark 9:35; 10:41-45

Andrew was open to truth and was ready to share that truth with others, introducing them to Jesus. Andrew modeled yet a third characteristic of discipleship. He was willing to serve Christ without fanfare. Note that while Andrew was the first disciple to respond to Jesus' call and the one who introduced his brother Simon Peter to Jesus, he is regularly referred to as "the brother of Simon Peter." Look at the list of disciples in Matthew 10:2 and Luke 6:14 and the reference to Andrew in John 6:8. These references suggest that by the time the Gospels were being written, this was the best way to identify Andrew. In other words, while people might not know about Andrew, they would certainly know about Peter.

Although Andrew did not receive much recognition in his own right, he was willing to step forward when needed and to step back when necessary. In short, he was willing to serve selflessly. His concern was to get the job done. So long as the mission was accomplished, he was not concerned with who got the credit. Clearly Andrew had come to understand and apply Jesus' teaching about the humility of servanthood: "Whoever wants to be first must be last of all and servant of all" (Mark 9:35; see 10:41-45).

Andrew's story is the story of all persons who labor in quiet humility, all of those whose concern is not the accolades of other people but the accomplishing of the will of God. This must always be the concern of the disciple of Jesus. "Your kingdom come. Your will be done, on earth as it is in heaven" (Matt 6:10). Are you willing to be an Andrew, committed to the accomplishing of God's purposes regardless of the reward? There is no limit to what God can do with that kind of commitment.

According to early Christian tradition, after the ascension of Jesus, Andrew was allotted the ancient territory of Scythia (a region north of the Black Sea between the River Danube and the River Tanais, which is part of modern Russia) as his mission field.[1] The Scythians, infamous in the ancient world for their barbarity, were said by Josephus to be "little different from wild beasts."[2] As a result of the traditions of his preaching there, Andrew came to be the patron saint of Russia. Other traditions indicate that he also preached in Cappadocia, Bithynia, Galatia, and Byzantium.

A late second-century document known as the *Acts of Andrew* tells of his ministry and subsequent martyrdom in Achaia (Greece). According to this account, Andrew was condemned to death by Aegeates, the governor of Patras, who was enraged because of the conversion of his wife Maximilla and his brother Stratocles. Aegeates ordered that Andrew be crucified. In order to prolong his agony, however, he ordered that rather than being nailed to the cross he be tied to the cross and left to die of hunger and thirst. As Andrew approached the cross, he prayed:

> Hail precious cross! Thou hast been consecrated by the body of my Lord, and adorned with his limbs as rich jewels. I come to thee exulting and glad. Receive me with joy into thy arms. O good cross, thou hast received beauty from our Lord's limbs. I have ardently loved thee. Long have I desired and sought thee. Now thou art found by me, and art made ready for my longing soul. Receive me into thy arms; take me up from among men, and present me to my Master, that he who redeemed me on thee may receive me by thee.[3]

After having been beaten with seven scourges, he was bound to the cross where he remained alive for two days preaching the gospel. Later tradition says he requested that his cross be in the shape of an "X" because he was unworthy to die on a cross shaped like his Lord's. These traditions suggest that Andrew died the way he had lived, humble and ever telling others about Jesus.

From Andrew, the first disciple Jesus called, we learn a great deal about what it means to journey with Jesus. To be Christ's disciple we must be open to truth wherever it may lead us and whatever the cost. We must be prepared to "come and see" what Jesus calls us to be and do. To be his disciple we must be ready and willing to introduce others to Jesus, any others and all others. To be his disciple we must be committed to the quiet humility of servanthood, ready to serve without fanfare, content when God's will is done. These characteristics clearly marked the life of Andrew. May it be said that they mark our lives too!

Notes

[1]Eusebius, *Ecclesiastical History*, 3.1.

[2]Josephus, *Against Apion*, 2.37.

[3]The prayer as quoted by William Barclay in *The Master's Men* (London: SCM, 1959) 42-43.

Peter

Biblical Texts
Matthew 16:13-23;
Mark 14:27-31, 66-71; 16:1-8; John 21:1-17

The New Testament tells us more about Peter than it does about any of the disciples of Jesus. While he is best known to us by his nickname ("Peter"), in the New Testament he is most frequently called by the name Simon, likely the name by which he was best known. According to the Gospels, Jesus gave him the nickname "Rock," which is *Cephas* in Aramaic and *Petras* (from which Peter comes) in Greek (Mark 3:16; Luke 6:14; John 1:42), and John characteristically refers to him as Simon Peter. His father was Jonah (Matt 16:17) or John (John 1:42), and he was the brother of Andrew, who introduced him to Jesus (John 1:40-42). He lived in the Galilean town of Capernaum on the northern shore of the Sea of Galilee where he and Andrew operated a fishing business. He was married (Mark 1:29-34; Matt 8:14-17) and, according to Paul, took his wife on some of his missionary journeys (1 Cor 9:5).

In all four Gospels, Peter is named as one of the first disciples to be called by Jesus. According to John 1:35-42, he first came into contact with Jesus through the preaching of John the Baptist in Judea. The Synoptics describe how at a later time Jesus found Peter, Andrew, James, and John fishing in the Sea of Galilee and called them to become "fishers of men." Peter and the others left everything to follow him. Peter's house in Capernaum appears to have served as a kind of headquarters during the early Galilean ministry, and on one occasion his boat served as a kind of floating pulpit (Luke 5:3).

Peter's name appears first in every list of the names of the twelve apostles in the New Testament, and he is portrayed as the leader of and spokesperson for the apostolic band (Matt 16:16; 19:27; Mark 8:29, 33; 10:28; Luke 9:20; 12:41; 18:28). In some cases, a question ascribed to "the disciples" in one Gospel is ascribed specifically to Peter in another (for example, compare Mark 7:17 and Matt 15:15). The prominent role of Peter is reflected where Peter is singled out while the other disciples are mentioned as a group associated with him (Mark 1:36; Luke 8:45; 9:32). When the inner circle of the Twelve is mentioned, Peter is always involved and mentioned first (Matt 17:1; 26:37; Mark 5:37; 9:2; 13:3; 14:33; Luke 5:10; 9:28; 22:8). He is most remembered for his epoch-making confession that Jesus is the Christ (Matt 16:16; Mark 8:29; Luke 9:20) and for his subsequent denial of Jesus (Matt 26:69-75; Mark 14:66-72; Luke 22:54-62).

Peter seems to have been a typical Galilean. Josephus, the first-century Jewish historian who was for a time the governor of Galilee and knew the residents well, described the Galileans as

> ever fond of innovations, and by nature disposed to changes, and delighted in seditions. . . . They were ever ready to follow a leader and to begin an insurrection.[1]

He also said that they were notoriously quick-tempered, given to quarreling, but never lacking in courage. Barclay suggested that this description, "Quick-tempered, impulsive, emotional, easily aroused by an appeal to adventure, loyal to the end—Peter was a typical man of Galilee."[2]

The early traditions about Peter suggest a close connection between Peter and Mark. In fact, Papias, who was the bishop of Hierapolis in the first half of the second century and an eager student of how the Gospels came to be written, suggested the following account of the writing of Mark's Gospel:

> Mark, having become the interpreter of Peter, wrote down accurately everything that he remembered, without however recording in order what was said or done by Christ. For neither did he hear the Lord speak, nor did he follow him, but afterwards, as I said, he followed Peter, who adapted his instruction to the need of his hearers, but had no design of giving a connected account of the Lord's oracles. So then Mark made no mistake while he thus wrote some things down as he remembered them, for he made it his one care not to omit anything that he had heard, or to set down any false statement therein.[3]

Thus, according to Papias, Mark's Gospel is basically a record of the preaching of Peter.

According to the unanimous tradition of the early church, Peter went to Rome, probably about 61 C.E. and was subsequently martyred there. Prior to this, tradition suggests that he preached in Asia Minor, a view that would seem to be supported by the Petrine correspondence that was addressed to churches there. Still another tradition says that he was the bishop of Antioch for seven years.[4]

Like most of us, Peter's life as a disciple was characterized by peaks and valleys, highs and lows, ups and downs. A look at several of the most significant events in Peter's life reveals a great deal about the nature of discipleship.

Peter's Great Discovery
Reflection Text
Matthew 16:13-20

The time of Jesus' ministry was drawing to a close. After months of preaching, teaching, and healing in Galilee, he had traveled north of Galilee with his disciples to a place called Caesarea Philippi. Caesarea Philippi had been built by Herod Philip, one of the sons of Herod the Great, to honor the reigning Roman caesar. It was a thoroughly Roman city and a significant center of pagan worship, especially the worship of Pan, the god of nature.

It was here, surrounded by the shrines of pagan deities, that Jesus addressed the ultimate question to his disciples: "Who do people say that the Son of Man is?" (Matt 16:13). The disciples answered by repeating a variety of suggestions that reflected current public opinion. Some of them believed Jesus to be John the Baptist. Others believed him to be Elijah or Jeremiah or one of the prophets. In Jesus' day, as in our own, there were many different perceptions about his identity. In the end, however, what other people think about Jesus does not matter. In the final analysis, we will be accountable for our own beliefs about him. We should not be surprised, therefore, when Jesus pressed the question home: "But who do *you* say that I am?" (v. 15).

Immediately Peter stepped forward and responded to Jesus' question with what has been called his great confession: "You are the Christ (the Greek term for messiah), the Son of the living God" (v. 16). According to the synoptic Gospels, Peter was the first person to make this confession, which has become the cornerstone of the church through the ages, for all who would enter the church must join Peter in making this great confession. No wonder Jesus said,

> Blessed are you, Simon son of Jonah. Flesh and blood has not revealed this to you but my father in heaven. And I tell you, you are Peter, and on this rock I will build my church. (vv. 17-18)

Perhaps this saying was in Peter's mind many years later when, in his first letter to the Christians of Asia Minor, he described his fellow believers as "living stones . . . built into a spiritual house" (1 Pet 2:5). Every Christian is a living stone in the edifice of the church, every person who has made Peter's great confession: "You are the Christ, the Son of the living God" (Matt 16:16).

The Great Rebuke
Reflection Text
Matthew 16:21-23

Immediately after Peter's great confession, Jesus began to teach his disciples that he must go up to Jerusalem, be handed over to the authorities, suffer, and die. Peter was shocked and horrified by this teaching. He could not conceive of such a possibility. The idea that the Messiah could suffer and die ran counter to everything he had ever been taught and everything he believed. All of his life he had been taught to expect a messiah who would come in great power and glory to deal death and destruction to the enemies of God's people. Jesus' talk of suffering and death just did not fit Peter's agenda.

In this incident Peter manifests clearly one of humanity's greatest problems in its relationship with God. From the beginning of time, human beings have wanted to set God's agenda. We want to decide what God can and cannot do, what God should and should not do. As long as God acts in ways that fit our agenda, we are quite satisfied, but we are not always ready and willing to accept the possibility that God may choose to act otherwise! Peter had definite preconceptions about who Jesus should be and what Jesus should do in order to be the Messiah. Suffering and death were not a part of that program. So Peter took Jesus aside in order to set him straight: "God forbid it, Lord! This must never happen to you" (Matt 16:22).

Jesus responded to Peter with a sharp rebuke: "Get behind me, Satan!" (v. 23). Satan? Have you ever wondered why Peter received such a sharp rebuke? The fact is, of course, that Peter was setting before Jesus the same temptation with which Satan had confronted Jesus during the days in the wilderness at the very beginning of his public ministry (Matt 4:1-11). In each of the three temptations Jesus faced there was, in essence, the temptation to be a different kind of messiah than that which God had set him to be, to take a different course of action to accomplish his messianic mission.

The temptation to turn stones into bread was the temptation to bid for people's loyalty by providing material blessings. The temptation to leap from the temple was the temptation to dazzle people with the sensational. The temptation to fall down and worship Satan was the temptation to compromise with the world's way. Thus, from the very beginning, Jesus was continually tempted to be another kind of messiah, to do his work another way—the way of the world, the way of power and glory—rather than the way of suffering and service. At Caesarea Philippi, Peter was presenting Jesus with that same temptation again.

In this incident, Peter stands before us as a clear example of the need for growth in the disciple's life. He had made his confession of faith. He had acknowledged that Jesus was the Christ, but he was far from the end of the journey of discipleship. In the days and weeks to follow he would come to see that the Messiah he had recognized and welcomed would be a very different kind of messiah than the one he had anticipated. He would come to see through some very painful experiences that the ways of God and humanity are not necessarily the same. They may, in fact, be very, very different. This growth would not be easy for Peter. We see him stumbling again and again after Caesarea Philippi. Nevertheless, this kind of continuing growth must characterize the life of a disciple of Jesus. The disciple's life is a continuing journey of faith and discovery in which one is challenged again and again to say, "Not my will but your will be done . . . wherever that may lead."

The Great Denial
Reflection Text
Mark 14:27-31, 66-71

The arrest of Jesus was imminent. He had shared a last supper with his disciples in the upper room. During the course of the meal Peter had announced his unbreakable loyalty to Jesus: "Even though I must die with you, I will not deny you" (Mark 14:31). When the supper was completed, Jesus and the disciples marched across the Kidron valley to the Garden of Gethsemane on the Mount of Olives. There the soldiers came and arrested Jesus, and then they took him to the house of Caiaphas. Peter followed along and soon found himself in the courtyard of Caiaphas' house, warming himself by a fire. Notice now the flow of the biblical narrative as presented by Mark.

In Mark 14:63-65, the focus falls clearly on Jesus. Standing before the high priest and his council, Jesus remained faithful to his identity and the mission that God had entrusted to him. The powers of this world could not dissuade him from his appointed task. In 14:66-71, the focus shifts to Peter. At the very same time Jesus was standing trial inside Caiaphas' house, Peter was outside in the courtyard. His Galilean accent betrayed him, and he was recognized as a follower of the Nazarene.

Then only a few hours after Peter had pledged undying loyalty to Jesus in the upper room, he was challenged to acknowledge that he was, indeed, one of Jesus' disciples. Three times he denied his identity as a disciple. Do you see the stark contrast that Mark has set before us? On the one hand we see the faithfulness of Jesus as he stood faithful to his identity and mission. On the other hand, we see the failure of Peter who denied his identity as Jesus' disciple!

Looking back on these events 2,000 years later, we wonder how Peter could so quickly deny his Lord, especially after the pledge of faithfulness he had so recently made before all of the disciples. Before the gavel of judgment falls, however, let us examine our own lives. We too have made bold commitments to Christ. Could our bold commitments possibly have gone unfulfilled?

Think back on the commitments that you have made to Christ—commitments to be more faithful in your daily life, to study God's Word more often and more carefully, to spend more time developing your relationship with God in prayer, to be more faithful in your participation in the life and ministry of his church. How faithful have you been to your commitments, your pledges of faithfulness to God? Peter is not the only one who has forsaken Jesus. Whenever we fail to do that which we have been called to do, whenever we fail to follow through on our commitments to Christ, we find ourselves standing with Peter in Caiaphas' courtyard. Our Lord stands faithful to us. What about our faithfulness to him?

Faithlessness can mark the lives of even the most committed at times. We must remember that even being in the courtyard of Caiaphas required of Peter a great deal of courage. He had, after all, struck the high priest's servant with his sword. Now he had come into the backyard of the one he had assaulted! Regardless of the danger, he had at least followed Jesus there. Without a doubt, Peter was a courageous man—only a courageous man would have been where Peter was. The other disciples had fled. Peter had followed this far, but even the most courageous, even the most committed may find themselves where Peter was: forsaking Jesus!

The Great Reconciliation
Reflection Texts
Mark 16:1-8; John 21:1-17

Peter's story does not end in Caiaphas' courtyard, however, because Jesus' story does not end there. Jesus was condemned, crucified, and buried, but even this is not the end. Mark tells how the women came to the tomb on the first day of the week to anoint Jesus' body. There they received the greatest news that has ever been heard:

> Do not be alarmed; you are looking for Jesus the Nazarene, who was crucified. He has been raised, he is not here. Look, there is the place they laid him. But go, tell his disciples and Peter that he is going ahead of you to Galilee; there you will see him, just as he told you. (16:6-7)

Do you notice anything interesting about the messenger's command to the women? "Go, tell his disciples *and Peter*." Now try to imagine how Peter must have felt after Jesus' death. He must have experienced not only the deep sadness that must have accompanied the loss of Jesus, but also the intense anguish of knowing that in the last hour he had denied his Lord. He had let his master down. Surely, he must have seen himself as a miserable failure as a disciple. How terrible he must have felt during those dark dreadful days after the crucifixion!

Then came the incredible news. Jesus was not dead—he was alive! How do you think Peter would have felt? After all, even if the news was true, and Jesus was alive, what possible use could Jesus have for a disciple who had failed him so miserably, one who had denied his identity as a disciple three times? The angelic messenger had anticipated Peter's feelings. He instructed the women to "tell his disciples *and Peter*." It is almost as if he was saying, "Be sure that Peter understands. . . . Jesus goes before *him* and calls *him* to follow too."

John 21 tells us of Peter's reunion with Jesus in Galilee. Interestingly, Peter had denied his Lord around a campfire, and there they met again. Jesus approached Peter with a question: "Simon son of John, do you love me?" (v. 15). Notice that Jesus put the question to Peter not once, not even twice, but three times. Three times Peter had denied his identity as a disciple of Jesus; three times Jesus gave Peter the opportunity to affirm his love and commitment once again. Thus, by the Sea of Galilee, Peter discovered "the forgiveness beyond reason which can meet the sin beyond excuse."[5]

This is the good news of Jesus Christ! The risen Christ calls us to be his disciples, and in that call he comes to meet us with his marvelous grace, love, and forgiveness. At times, we, like Peter, will stumble and fall. Like Peter at Caesarea Philippi, we will fail to make Christ's will our will. Like Peter in Caiaphas' courtyard, we will fail to fulfill our commitments to our Lord. Still he goes before us and calls us on to follow him, the living Lord who meets us with his grace, love, and forgiveness all along the way.

Peter responded to the grace. He accepted the commission of the risen Lord to feed his sheep and spent the rest of his life in his service. As we have said, according to the unanimous tradition of the early church, Peter went to Rome and died as a martyr there—faithful unto death. It is said that when his life was threatened in Rome, he was warned and encouraged by the members of the church there to seek safety by fleeing the city. As he was fleeing, however, he met the Lord who was entering the city. "Lord," he asked, "Whither goest thou" (*Domine, quo vadis*)? The Lord answered, "I go to Rome to be crucified." "Lord," said Peter, "art thou being crucified again?" "Yes, Peter, I am being crucified again." Peter understood that Jesus was going into Rome to bear the cross from which he was running. He turned back and entered the city to die for his Lord.

According to tradition, Peter's wife was crucified before his eyes while he, being forced to look on, encouraged her to "remember the Lord."[6] When the time for his own crucifixion came, Peter requested that he might be crucified upside down since he felt that he was not worthy to die as his Lord had died, and he conducted himself with such courage that even his jailer was moved to become a Christian.

Peter, O Peter! His was a life of highs and lows, of peaks and valleys. Such is the way for all of us. Like Peter we hear the call of Jesus, we struggle to follow, and again and again he comes to lift us up and call us on to an even greater understanding of his will and a greater faithfulness to our call.

Notes

[1]Josephus, *Life*, 17; *Jewish War*, 3.3.2.
[2]William Barclay, *The Master's Men* (London: SCM, 1959) 19.
[3]Quoted in Eusebius, *Ecclesiastical History*, 3.39.15.
[4]Eusebius, *Ecclesiastical History*. 3.1.2; 3.36.2
[5]Barclay, 21.
[6]Eusebius, *Ecclesiastical History*, 3.30.

Nathanael
Bartholomew

Biblical Texts
Matthew 10:3; Mark 3:18; Luke 6:14; John 1:43-51; Acts 1:13

In every list of the twelve apostles in the New Testament, we find the mention of an apostle named Bartholomew. Unfortunately, the Gospels that contain these lists tell us nothing else about this Bartholomew. For centuries, however, students of the New Testament have suggested that this person is to be identified with Nathanael in the Gospel of John. One ancient tradition describes him as follows:

> He has black, curly hair, white skin, large eyes, straight nose, his hair covers his ears, his beard long and grizzled, middle height. He wears a white robe with a purple stripe, and a white cloak with four purple gems at the corners. For twenty-six years he has worn these, and they never grow old. His shoes have lasted twenty-six years. He prays a hundred times a day and a hundred times a night. His voice is like a trumpet; angels wait upon him; he is always cheerful, and knows all languages.[1]

Several suggestions regarding Nathanael's identity have been offered through the years. A number of inferior manuscripts of the New Testament call Simon by the name Kananites. Assuming that this meant "man of Cana" and noting that Nathanael was from Cana (John 21:2), some scholars have suggested that Nathanael and Simon were the same person. Epiphanius, a fourth-century bishop of Salamis and a native of Palestine, identified Nathanael with the unnamed disciple on the Emmaus Road (Luke 24:13-25).[2] Other researchers have identified Nathanael with the "beloved disciple" of the Gospel of John based on Jesus' description of Nathanael as "an Israelite in whom there is no deceit [guile]" (John 1:47).

Most ingenious perhaps is the identification of Nathanael with Stephen, based on Jesus' promise to Nathanael that he would see the heavens open and the angels of God ascending and descending upon the Son of Man (John 1:51). According to the account of Stephen's martyrdom, he saw the heavens opened and Jesus standing at the right hand of God (Acts 7:5b). As interesting as these suggestions may be, however, the most likely identification is that Nathanael of the Gospel of John was, in fact, the Bartholomew of the Synoptics.

A number of factors seem to support this longstanding view. Bartholomew is not a first name, but rather a family name used to distinguish a person by identifying that person with his father. In Aramaic, the word *bar* means "son of." Thus, Jesus referred to Simon Peter as "Simon bar Jona," that is, "Simon, son of Jona." Bartholomew means "son of Tolmai" or "Talmai." For people to come to be called by this second name was not uncommon. Think, for example, of Bartimaeus ("son of Timaeus") and Barabbas ("son of the father"). Possibly Bartholomew was the second name of this apostle, by which he came to be known to some people. What then was his first name?

Note that Bartholomew is not mentioned in the Gospel of John. We are, however, introduced to Nathanael, who is placed in the company of the apostles and appears to be a friend of Philip. In fact, Philip introduced Nathanael to Jesus. A review of the lists of the apostles in Matthew, Mark, and Luke reveals that Philip and Bartholomew always appeared together as if it was natural to think of them together. Taken together, this evidence suggests that Bartholomew and Nathanael are two names borne by the same person: a man named Nathanael (which means "gift of God") Bartholomew ("son of Tolmai" or "Talmai"). While Matthew, Mark, and Luke tell us nothing about Nathanael, he is mentioned in John 21:2 and plays a major role in John 1:43-51. An examination of this passage reveals him to be a person who demonstrated a number of significant qualities that should characterize a disciple of Jesus.

Commitment to the Study of God's Word
Reflection Text
John 1:43-51

According to John 21:2, Nathanael was from the city of Cana in Galilee. John 1:43 tells us that when Jesus decided to go to Galilee, he found Philip and called him to follow. Philip immediately found Nathanael and shared with him his discovery that Jesus was the Messiah. Though Philip was from Bethsaida (across the Sea of Galilee from Cana), he and Nathanael had apparently become close friends, friends who anxiously awaited the coming of the long-expected Messiah. Notice the way Philip approached Nathanael when he came to tell him about Jesus: "We have found him about whom Moses in the law and also the prophets wrote" (John 1:45). Clearly, Philip assumed that Nathanael knew the witness of Moses in the Law and the witness of the prophets concerning the coming Messiah. In other words, Nathanael was a student of the Scriptures.

Perhaps Philip's assumption reflects the possibility that he and Nathanael had spent long hours together searching the Scriptures for insights about the promised Messiah and his coming. Whether this be the case or not, the clear implication of Philip's statement is that Nathanael was both anxiously expecting the Messiah and well-versed in the Scriptures that spoke of the Messiah. He was a man committed to the study of God's Word. Perhaps this is why he was able to recognize Jesus as the Messiah once he met him. His study of God's Word had made him sensitive to the voice of God and enabled him to recognize how God's purposes were being worked out in and through Jesus.

This is the call of every disciple: to hear the call of God and commit ourselves to the working out of God's purposes in us and through us. There is no substitute for the study of God's Word in our attempts to be faithful to that divine call. As we study the Scriptures, we are able to become more sensitive to this call, and our eyes are continually opened to recognize the ways God is at work in the world.

Commitment to Prayer
Reflection Text
John 1:48-51

In John 1:48-50, Jesus surprises Nathanael by announcing that he has seen him sitting under the fig tree. Though often overlooked, this little detail may be very important for understanding Nathanael. The fig tree in Palestine normally grows to a height of about fifteen feet, and its branches may spread as much as twenty-five feet. Planted near a house, it came to be seen as providing a kind of extra room, especially for the poor whose houses usually had but one room. In fact, the fig tree had become an important place for the study of scripture, and often a rabbi would sit with his pupils and discuss the Torah there. This may have led to the tradition that Nathanael was himself a scribe. The fig tree also became an important place for prayer and meditation. Thus, when Jesus revealed to Nathanael that he had seen him sitting beneath the fig tree, he may have been saying: "Nathanael, I have seen you at prayer in your private devotion."

Nathanael was a man of prayer. He sought the Lord not only through the study of the Word, but also in prayer. Perhaps this also helps to explain why he was able to recognize Jesus as the Messiah. As William Barclay said, "When the light of study is warmed by the fire of devotion, then indeed discoveries are made."[3] As disciples, we too must be people of prayer. It has often been suggested that Satan trembles when he sees a Christian in prayer. This statement must be true, for prayer is our avenue of personal communion with God. As we pray, we come to know God better, which leads us to more faithful service. Disciples of Jesus must be people who pray. In his classic book *Quiet Talks on Prayer,* S. D. Gordon wrote:

> The great people of the earth today are people who pray. I do not mean those who talk about prayer; nor those who can explain about prayer; but I mean those who *take* time and *pray*. They have not the time. It must be taken from something else. This something else is important—very important and pressing, but still less important and less pressing than prayer.[4]

Commitment to the Truth
Reflection Text
John 1:47

Jesus' description of Nathanael in John 1:47 is suggestive of another of his characteristics: "Here is truly an Israelite in whom there is no deceit [guile]." Jesus recognized in Nathanael a genuine sincerity and a deep-seated commitment to Judaism. Perhaps this was a way of acknowledging Nathanael's desire to be as faithful to Judaism as possible. He was committed to the God of Israel, committed to the study of the Scriptures of Israel, and committed to the coming of the Messiah of Israel. His commitment was not merely cosmetic—not like make-up, which is not really part of us but we put on to make us look different to others. There was no guile in Nathanael, no hypocrisy, no deceit. Here was an honest, sincere, deeply committed Jew.

In Romans 9:6 Paul states that "not all Israelites truly belong to Israel." In Romans 2:28-29 he makes a distinction that is perhaps appropriate to recall here:

> For a person is not a Jew who is one outwardly, nor is true circumcision something external and physical. Rather, a person is a Jew who is one inwardly, and real circumcision is a matter of the heart.

Nathanael was an Israelite who was of Israel. He was not just a Jew outwardly but inwardly too. The psalmist said that a true son of Israel is one "in whose spirit there is no deceit" (Ps 32:2). Nathanael was such a one as this.

In spite of all his strengths, Nathanael also manifested a quality that could have destroyed him. Do you remember his response to Philip when Philip first approached him with the news about Jesus? Nathanael said, "Can anything good come out of Nazareth?" (John 1:46). This response reflected a clear prejudice towards the people of Nazareth. Nazareth and Cana were neighboring villages. During the time of Jesus, however, Nazareth was a very small and insignificant village—so insignificant, in fact, that the first-century Jewish historian Josephus did not even include it in his list of the towns and villages of Galilee! Cana, on the other hand, was a much more significant town. Nathanael reflected the kind of prejudice that often rears its ugly head between members of neighboring communities.

Webster defines prejudice as a

> preconceived judgment or opinion . . . without just grounds or before sufficient knowledge . . . an irrational attitude of hostility directed against an individual, a group, a race or their supposed characteristics.[5]

Such an attitude can quickly and easily become a part of our way of thinking. It feeds on the human desire to see ourselves as superior to others. Such prejudice can easily blind us so that we are no longer able to see or to be open to others. It can prevent us from seeing God's truth and sharing that truth with others.

A second attitude reflected in Nathanael's response is the tendency to become enslaved to our presuppositions and preconceptions. Nathanael's skepticism with regard to Jesus stemmed from his preconceived notion that the Messiah could not possibly be from Nazareth. The popular notion among first-century Jews was that the Messiah would be born and grow up in Bethlehem. No doubt Nathanael felt that anyone who studied the Scriptures would know that. Furthermore, Nazareth is never mentioned in any prophetic word about the Messiah. In fact, it is not mentioned at all in the Old Testament! Jesus could not be the Messiah and be from Nazareth—especially Nazareth! Thus, Nathanael's presuppositions and preconceptions about the Messiah almost prevented him from recognizing the Messiah. He was so convinced that he knew the truth that he almost missed it!

Fortunately, Philip's persistence and his challenge to Nathanael to "come and see" Jesus for himself prompted Nathanael to look beyond his prejudices and presuppositions to see that God is not limited by our notions of who God is and what God can and cannot do. Throughout the Bible we see again and again that God's ways are not humanity's ways. We must constantly be open to the fact that God is not limited to our presuppositions and preconceptions about God. Still there remains a great desire to put God in a box of our own design and construction.

Many years ago J. B. Phillips wrote a marvelous little book called *Your God Is Too Small.* In this book he strikes at the heart of the matter. Simply put: we must let God be God! As his disciples, Jesus calls us to be a people who are willing to let our presuppositions and preconceptions be shaped and reshaped as we, like Nathanael, "come and see" who Jesus is and how he is at work in our lives and in the world around us. Indeed, as we open our eyes to see and open our ears to hear, bringing a sincere commitment to the study of God's Word and the deepening of our relationship to Christ through prayer, we, like Nathanael, will exclaim "You are the Son of God." Like Nathanael, we will want to give ourselves in total surrender to his lordship. Nathanael was so committed to knowing the truth that he was willing to go wherever it led him, even when that meant confronting his prejudices and going against his presuppositions and preconceptions. Once he discovered that truth, he committed himself to it totally.

Early Christian tradition depicts Nathanael as having a significant ministry in a number of settings. According to Eusebius and Jerome, when Pantaenus (a famous Stoic philosopher who was converted to Christianity in the latter part of the second century) went from Alexandria to India, he found Christians there who possessed a Hebrew version of Matthew's Gospel.

> For Bartholomew, one of the apostles, had preached to them and left
> them with the writing of Matthew in the Hebrew language, which
> they had preserved till that time.[6]

Another tradition preserved in the *Acts of Philip* says that Nathanael traveled to Scythia and Hieropolis with Philip. Both men were arrested and condemned to be crucified. Nathanael escaped, however, and traveled to Armenia where he continued his ministry. While there he healed the daughter of the king and demonstrated the impotency of the king's idols. This so infuriated the pagan priests that, with the help of the king's brother, they had him executed in 68 C.E. According to the tradition, he was beaten with clubs, skinned alive, crucified, and then beheaded! If this tradition is true, it bears witness to the fact that once Nathanael discovered the truth, he committed himself to it totally.

The disciple of Jesus in today's world can do no less than what Nathanael did. We must be committed to the study of God's Word. We must be committed to the deepening of our relationship to God in prayer. We must be committed to God's truth whatever it may be and wherever it may lead. We must be committed to surrender our lives completely to the Jesus who is the Son of God. In short, we must be prepared to say with the hymn writer of old: "All to Jesus I surrender, All to Him I freely give!"

Notes

[1]This description comes from *The Apostolic History of Abdias*, which is usually dated to the latter half of the fourth century.

[2]Epiphanius, *Heresies*, 23.

[3]William Barclay, *The Master's Men* (London: SCM, 1959) 112.

[4]S. D. Gordon, *Quiet Talks on Prayer* (New York: Grosset & Dunlap, 1941) 12-13.

[5]*Webster's Ninth New Collegiate Dictionary* (Springfield MA: Merriam-Webster, Inc., 1988) 928.

[6]Eusebius, *Ecclesiastical History*, 5.10.3. See also Jerome, *Concerning Illustrious Men*, 36.

Judas
Son of James

Biblical Texts
Matthew 10:3; Mark 3:18;
Luke 6:16; John 14:15-31; Acts 1:13

Did you know that two disciples of Jesus bore the name Judas? There was, of course, Judas Iscariot. We are all familiar with him. There was also Judas, the son of James, about whom we know very little. His name appears in the list of the Twelve in Luke 6:16 and Acts 1:13. In John 14:22, we find a reference to "Judas" (not Iscariot), thus making clear the distinction between the two apostles who bore the same name. In Mark 3:18 and in the earliest versions of Matthew 10:3, he is called Thaddeus, though some later versions of Matthew 10:3 refer to him as "Lebbaeus, called Thaddeus." Interestingly, Jerome, a fourth-century church historian, called him "Trinomius," which means "a man with three names!"[1]

Most likely, Judas was the given name of this apostle. It is a common Hebrew name meaning "Yahweh leads." Both Thaddeus and Lebbaeus probably represent nicknames. Thaddeus seems to be derived from the Hebrew root *thed,* which means "breast." It may be a term of endearment such as "dear one," or, as some have suggested, it may carry the significance of "bold one" or "courageous one." Lebbaeus is derived from the Hebrew root for heart, *leb,* and would also seem to be a term of endearment. After the betrayal of Jesus by the other Judas, this Judas or those around him may have chosen to emphasize these nicknames over his given name. One could certainly understand why.

In the Greek text of Luke 6:16 and Acts 1:13, Judas is simply called "Judas of James." While the King James Version assumes this to mean Judas, the brother of James (note that the words "brother of" are in italics in the KJV, indicating that they are not found in the Greek text but were added by the translators), more modern translations render this "son of James," since the practice of the time was to identify persons with their father.

The New Testament tells us almost nothing about this Judas. Apart from one incident in John's Gospel where he is referred to as "Judas" (not Iscariot), he appears only in the lists of the Twelve. An early tradition suggests that he was a Zealot. Several manuscripts of *The Apostolic Constitution* (a fourth-century document from Syria) refer to "Thaddeus, also called Lebbaeus, who was surnamed 'Judas the Zealot'."[2] Support for this tradition has been found by some scholars in the question that Judas addressed to Jesus in the upper room. This question has been interpreted as Judas' plea to Jesus to make public his messiahship and fulfill the popular messianic expectations of a political and military messiah. The fact that he is always listed together with Simon the Zealot and Judas Iscariot (who is believed by some to have been a Zealot) has been seen as further evidence that Judas may also have been a member of this movement.

The only incident in which we meet Judas in Scripture is found in John 14:21-24. It was the night of Jesus' arrest, and the disciples had gathered with Jesus in the upper room. The Gospel of John records a long discussion between Jesus and his disciples as he tried to prepare them for the events of the following days. He announced that he was going to leave them (v. 19), but that he would not leave them empty-handed. In fact, he would come to them in the form of the Holy Spirit, not just to be with them, but to dwell within them (vv. 16-18, 25-26). In this context Judas asked Jesus a question—a question that may tell us something about Judas and a question that prompted an answer from Jesus that is of great significance for all who would be his disciples.

Judas' Question
Reflection Text
John 14:22

The news that Jesus would leave the disciples was particularly perplexing for Judas, as was Jesus' promise that while the world would see him no more, he would manifest himself to his disciples (John 14:18-21). Notice his question to Jesus: "Lord, how is it that you will reveal yourself to us, and not to the world?" (v. 22). The emphasis of the Greek form of the question really falls on "why" rather than on "how." Judas was asking Jesus why he would not manifest himself to the world. Why was Jesus' statement so baffling to Judas? Why did he not understand what Jesus was trying to say?

The tradition that Judas was a Zealot may be helpful at this point. If this tradition is true, then Judas was an ardent Jewish nationalist, a super patriot who never accepted the rule of Rome and lived for the day when the yoke of Roman bondage would be broken. Popular messianic expectation included the belief that the Messiah would be God's agent for accomplishing this deliverance. Jesus' disciples had come to believe that Jesus was the long-awaited Messiah, and this could only mean one thing for anyone with Zealot leanings. As Messiah, Jesus would be the one to bring about this deliverance from Roman bondage.

Perhaps Judas, like so many of Jesus' followers, lived in anticipation of the day when Jesus would publicly declare his messiahship and restore Israel to its former freedom, greatness, and power. The Romans would be driven into the sea, and Israel would judge and govern the nations. But now Jesus was talking about going away and in the future manifesting himself to those who were his disciples. How, then, Judas wondered, could the Romans be driven out and the Kingdom established? "Why reveal yourself to us (we know who you are!) and not to the world (they're the ones who need to know!)?"

Jesus' Response
Reflection Text
John 14:23-24

We should be grateful for Judas' dilemma and the question it prompted, for Jesus' response contains some very significant truths for his disciples of every age. Notice that Judas' question in John 14:22 seems to have been prompted by Jesus' statement in verse 21 that he would manifest himself to those who love him. Verse 21 is an incredibly important one. In it Jesus basically says, "I can tell who loves me by the way they obey me, and I will reveal myself only to those who truly love and obey me." To put it another way, Jesus said that if someone claims to love God but doesn't obey God, that claim is a lie and Jesus will not reveal himself to that person.

Judas assumed that Jesus' reference to revealing himself was a reference to his revealing himself as Messiah, which would mean setting up an earthly kingdom over which Jesus would reign as king. He was unable to understand the meaning of Jesus' words because his preconceptions would not allow for any other kind of kingdom. Jesus was speaking of another kind of kingdom, however. His kingdom would not be defined by geography or time but would exist wherever and whenever God rules in the hearts of human beings. We become citizens of this kind of kingdom by obedience to its king. Since Judas obviously did not understand what Jesus was saying, Jesus repeated the same principle again in verses 23-24:

> Jesus answered him, "Those who love me will keep my word, and my Father will love them, and we will come to them and make our home with them. Whoever does not love me does not keep my words; and the word that you hear is not mine, but is from the father who sent me."

Jesus' word to Judas is a word for all times and places. The only people who are able to perceive Jesus are the ones who love him, and loving him means obedience to his will. Do you remember Jesus' words in the Sermon on the Mount?

> Not everyone who says to me, "Lord, Lord" will enter the kingdom of heaven, but only the one who does the will of my Father in heaven. Everyone then who hears these words of mine and acts on them will be like a wise man who built his house on rock. (Matt 7:21, 24)

Jesus' call to us is to do his will, to keep his commandments. "If you love me, you will keep my commandments" (John 14:15). He did not say "you may," or "you might," or "if it is not too inconvenient, how about giving it a try." He said "you will keep my commandments."

In his book *A Testament of Devotion,* Thomas Kelly wrote of the need for what he calls "holy obedience" in the life of the Christian:

> Meister Eckhart wrote: "There are plenty to follow our Lord halfway, but not the other half. They will give up possessions, friends, and honors, but it touches them too closely to disown themselves. It is just this astonishing life which is willing to follow Him the other half, sincerely to disown itself, this life which intends complete obedience, without any reservations, that I would propose to you in all humility, in all boldness, in all seriousness. I mean this literally, utterly, completely, and I mean it for you and for me—commit your lives in unreserved obedience to Him."

Kelly goes on to describe the results of such obedience:

> The life that intends to be wholly obedient, wholly submissive, wholly listening, is astonishing in its completeness. Its joys are ravishing, its peace profound, its humility the deepest, its power world-shaking, its love enveloping, its simplicity that of a trusting

child. It is the life and power in which the prophets and apostles lived. It is the life and power of Jesus of Nazareth, who knew that "when thine eye is single thy whole body is full of light" (Luke 11:34). It is the life and power of the apostle Paul, who resolved not to know anything among men save Jesus Christ and Him crucified. . . . it is the life and power of myriads of unknown saints through the ages. . . . And it is a life and power that can break forth in this tottering Western culture and return the Church to its rightful life as a fellowship of creative, heaven-led souls.[3]

The promise of Jesus to Judas is his promise to disciples of every age. As we do the will of God, God's revelation comes to us. We will recognize where God is at work in the world, and then we can join in that work.

One of Jesus' beatitudes provides an important insight at this point: "Blessed are the pure in heart, for they shall see God" (Matt 5:8). While we often assume that the promise of this beatitude relates to the future, we must recognize that while it does have eschatological implications, it relates to the present as well. The "pure in heart" will see God in the present! What then does it mean to be "pure in heart"?

Purity of heart is to be single-minded. It is to have a singleness of purpose in our lives. To have a pure heart is to have a life that is fixed on one thing. As a great Christian thinker of the last century put it, "Purity of heart is to will one thing."[4] It is to "strive first for the kingdom of God and his righteousness" (Matt 6:33). To be pure in heart is to be completely surrendered to God's purposes. When we are willing to do this, we will see where the Kingdom is making itself known in our world. We will see the King at work, and then we will be able to join in that work.

Jesus instructed Judas that if he wanted to know why Jesus was doing as he did, he must manifest a love for Jesus that was demonstrated by obedience. Love and obedience are the key words: "If you love me, you will keep my commandments." This is God's will for the disciple. So often we are concerned about the discovery of God's will for our lives. Most of the time, however, we are interested in a revelation about God's will for our future. What about God's will for the present? How much of God's will do we already know, and what is the measure of our obedience to that will? Think about these questions in relationship to your own life:

—Are you doing what you know to be God's will with regard to your study of the Word?

—Are you doing what you know to be God's will in relation to your prayer life?

—Are you doing what you know to be God's will in relation to your commitment to the church?

—Are you doing what you know to be God's will in relation to your witness?

—Are you doing what you know to be God's will in relation to your personal relationships?

—Are you doing what you know to be God's will in relation to your stewardship?

Perhaps the reason that Jesus does not manifest himself in our lives is that we simply are not willing to be obedient to what we already know his will to be. The fact is that we know enough of God's will to keep us busy every day that we live for as long as we live, but are we faithful to do what we know? Are we obedient? The promise that Jesus made to Judas is a promise to disciples in every age. He will reveal himself. He will make himself known to those who love him and keep his commandments. It is a promise that reminds us that for the disciple of Jesus, obedience is not a luxury nor an option, but the essential key to a vital Christian life.

According to early Christian tradition, Judas' life was marked by continuing obedience after the ascension of Jesus. Indeed, if the tradition is accurate, it was an obedience unto death. The tradition is a fascinating one, for it contains references to a supposed correspondence between Jesus and a king of Edessa named Abgarus, which Eusebius claims to have seen in the archive of Edessa.[5] According to Eusebius, Abgarus sent the following letter to Jesus:

> Abgarus, ruler of Edessa, to Jesus the excellent Savior who had appeared in the country of Jerusalem, greeting. I have heard the reports of thee and of thy cures as performed by thee without medicine and without herbs. For it is said that thou makest the blind to see and the lame to walk, that thou cleanest lepers and casteth out impure spirits and demons, and that thou healest those afflicted with lingering disease, and raisest the dead. And having heard all these things concerning thee, I have concluded that one of two things must be true: either thou art God, and having come down from heaven thou doest these things or else, thou who doest these things art the

Son of God. I have therefore written to thee to ask thee that thou wouldst take the trouble to come to me and heal the disease which I have. For I have heard that the Jews are murmuring against thee. But I have a very small yet noble city which is big enough for us both.

Eusebius also related the following letter of response from Jesus to Abgarus:

Blessed art thou who hast believed in me without having seen me. For it is written concerning me that they who have seen me will not believe in me, and that those who have not seen me will believe and be saved. But in regard to what thou hast written to me, that I should come to thee, it is necessary for me to fulfill all things here for which I have been sent, and after I have fulfilled them to be taken up again to him who sent me. But after I have been taken up I will send to thee one of my disciples, that he may heal thy disease, and give life to thee and to thine.

According to tradition, after Jesus' ascension, Thomas sent Thaddeus to Edessa where he healed many people. Abgarus called Thaddeus before him in order to determine if he was the disciple whom Jesus had sent. In response to his query, Thaddeus said,

Because thou hast mightily believed in him that sent me, therefore have I been sent unto thee. And still further, if thou believest in him, the petitions of thy heart shall be granted unto thee, as thou believest.

Abgarus responded,

So much have I believed in him that I wished to take an army and destroy those Jews who crucified him, if I had not been deterred by reason of the dominion of the Romans.

Thaddeus healed Abgarus, who asked him to tell him everything about Jesus. Thaddeus asked him to call the citizens of the city together so that he might tell them all.

I will preach in their presence, and sow among them the word of God, concerning the coming of Jesus, how he was born; and concerning his mission, for what purpose he was sent by the Father; and concerning the power of his works, and the mysteries which he proclaimed in the world, and by what power he did these things; and concerning his new preaching, and his abasement and humiliation, and how he humbled himself, and died and debased his divinity and was crucified, and descended into Hades, and burst the bars which from eternity had not been broken, and raised the dead; for he descended alone and rose with many, and thus ascended to his Father.

Abgarus' subsequent conversion brought such confusion to the kingdom that one of his nephews had Thaddeus imprisoned and put to death. If the tradition is true, then this disciple counted the cost of obedience and was willing to pay the price. May God grant that we may so faithfully follow our Lord in trusting obedience in our journey with Jesus.

Notes

[1]Jerome, *Homily on Matthew*, 10.4.

[2]Several Old Latin manuscripts (Vercellinus, Veronensis, Claromontanus, Sangermanesis), which range in date from the fourth to the ninth centuries, refer to this Judas as "Judas the Zealot" as does the *Epistola Apostolorum*.

[3]Thomas Kelly, *A Testament of Devotion* (New York: Harper & Row, 1941) 52.

[4]This famous dictum comes from the pen of Søren Kierkegaard in an essay entitled "Purity of Heart Is to Will One Thing" in "Edifying Discourses in Various Spirits" first written in 1847 and contained in *A Kierkegaard Anthology*, ed. Robert Bretall (New York: The Modern Library, 1946) 271.

[5]Eusebius, *Ecclesiastical History*, 1.13.

Philip

Biblical Texts
Matthew 10:3; Mark 3:18; Luke 6:14;
John 1:43-46; 6:1-14; 12:20-22; 14:8-11; Acts 1:13

If you ask many people about the apostle Philip, you are likely to get an answer that goes something like this: "Philip the apostle? Oh, yes, I remember him. He's the one who baptized the Ethiopian eunuch on the road to Gaza and preached to the Samaritans. Right?"

Wrong! There are two Philips in the New Testament: Philip the apostle and Philip the evangelist (or deacon). The problem is that we know more about Philip the evangelist (or deacon) than we do about Philip the apostle. Philip the evangelist was the Philip of Acts 6:5 who was one of the seven chosen to minister to the needs of the Hellenist widows in Jerusalem. He went to Samaria and preached the gospel (Acts 8:4-13) and was led by the Spirit to the Ethiopian eunuch (vv. 26-40). He hosted Paul in Caesarea, and his unmarried daughters prophesied (Acts 21:7-9), but he was not the apostle Philip! Yet, Philip the apostle and Philip the evangelist have been confused since the second century when the church father Tertullian wrote about the apostle Philip being snatched away from the Ethiopian eunuch.[1] That this confusion continues is not surprising. Our attention is focused on the apostle Philip. Just what do we know about this early disciple of Jesus?

According to John 1:43, Philip was from Bethsaida, the home of Peter and Andrew. Bethsaida, which means "fish house," was a busy, thriving community located on the northern shore of the Sea of Galilee. Herod Philip, one of the sons of Herod the Great who ruled the territory east and northeast of the Sea of Galilee from 4 B.C.E. until 34 C.E., had raised it to the status of a city, increased its population, and made it his capital city. Possibly Philip was named for this respected ruler who brought economic prosperity to his hometown and was known as one who administered justice fairly. At any rate, Philip bore a Greek name that means "lover of horses."

Beyond the pages of the New Testament are many traditions about Philip. While some traditions associate him with Carthage, Gaul, Lydia, and Parthia, the strongest tradition associates him with Asia Minor. Polycrates of Ephesus, writing about 190 C.E., describes Philip

as one of the "great lights" of Asia Minor.[2] One of the strongest traditions says that Philip went to Hieropolis, a city in Asia Minor near
Colossae and Laodicea, where he was martyred because he refused to
deny Christ. He was stripped naked, hung on a hook upside down by
his feet, and his ankles were pierced so that he would bleed to death
slowly. He had only one request: that his body be wrapped in papyrus
rather than linen, for he felt that his body should not be treated as the
body of his Lord.[3]

While Philip only appears in the lists of the twelve apostles in
Matthew, Mark, and Luke, he figures prominently in four significant
scenes in the Gospel of John. Each of these scenes reveals something
about Philip and the meaning of discipleship.

A Missionary Heart
Reflection Text
John 1:43-46

While the story of Philip's first meeting with Jesus is very brief, it is a
marvelous presentation of the most basic truths of Christianity. First, it
demonstrates the essence of the gospel. Notice that Jesus found Philip
(John 1:43). The story becomes a parable of the Good News that in
Jesus Christ, God has come for us. So the apostle Paul wrote that "in
Christ God was reconciling the world to himself" (2 Cor 5:19). This
message distinguishes Christianity from the other religions of the
world. In other religions humanity seeks to find God, but the Christian
gospel proclaims that God has come to find us and has also provided a
way by which we might live once again in that fellowship with God for
which we were created. God has taken the initiative on our behalf.
"While we were still sinners Christ died for us. . . . While we were enemies, we were reconciled to God through the death of his son" (Rom
5:8, 10). This is the Good News! Jesus came to find us just as he found
Philip. This is the essence of the gospel.

Second, this story presents the essence of discipleship. Jesus' call
to Philip was clear and succinct: "Follow me!" According to Mark's
Gospel, it is the same call that Jesus addressed to Peter and Andrew
(1:17). It is, in fact, the basic definition of discipleship given in the
Gospel narratives. Discipleship means following Jesus. To be a disciple means more than giving mental assent to a certain set of
propositions or just having a certain kind of emotional response. To be
a disciple of Jesus means to follow Jesus wherever he may call us to

go. Remember Jesus' words to his disciples as he made his way to Jerusalem: "If any want to become my followers, let them deny themselves and take up their cross and follow me" (Mark 8:34). Jesus made it clear to Philip from the very beginning: the essence of discipleship is following him. His call has not changed.

Notice Philip's response to this meeting with Jesus. The moment he found Christ he was determined to share Christ with others. He went immediately to find his friend Nathanael. In our study of Nathanael we suggested the possibility that Philip and Nathanael had studied the Scriptures together and waited together for the coming of the promised Messiah. Imagine the thrill Philip must have experienced when the opportunity came to share with his friend the news that this Messiah had come at last.

Clearly Philip had a missionary heart—his first inclination was to share the Good News with others, and he thought first of his friends! What a marvelous example he provided for disciples of every age. Philip was the pioneer of "friendship evangelism." It has been said that friendship provides the most fertile soil for evangelism, for within friendships the reality of Christ is introduced into a relationship of love that is already established. But do we share the Good News with our unsaved friends?

We must share the gospel both with those we know and those we do not know, but is it not reasonable to suggest that those we know should be at the top of our list of concern? Should we not be concerned to share the Good News with those people we already care about? Philip was! Are we? Perhaps our problem is that we do not know many unsaved people. Ask yourself this question. "How many unsaved friends do I have?"

A former director of evangelism for a Baptist state convention once suggested that most church members could count the number of unsaved friends they had on the fingers of one hand! Could he possibly have been right? If genuine evangelism is born out of relationships with others, should we not be seeking to know and care for those around us who need to find Christ? Philip was concerned to share Christ with others. What is the level of our concern?

In his book *The Church and the New Order,* William Paton tells the following story:

> A year ago I was ill in a New Jersey hospital and my doctor (who had been a missionary) was talking with me about the difference . . . between the all-out keenness with which medical resources were

mobilized for the very humblest and the apathy of Christians in the Christian cause. He said that a few nights before a Negro had come into the hospital, dangerously wounded after a drunken fracas. He was a known bully, and dying of a knife-wound in his belly. But the hospital, though it had no hope of saving him and though he was a drunken ne'er-do-well of whom society might deem itself well rid, used its most expensive methods for him and did for him all that it could have done for anyone—and this out of professional loyalty and keenness. My doctor wished that Christians and churches were as unlimited in their sacrifice and their commitment.

Paton concluded the following:

Of course, the reason [that we are not] is that we do not really believe. We assent, but we do not *believe*. When men really believe that the Son of God died for the sins of men and that through him we are brought into that kind of family relation to the Creator of all the worlds which is typified in Christ's use of the word "Abba," they do not keep the news to themselves.[4]

Could Paton be right? Do we really believe this Good News? If we did, would we not go to any length to share it with others? Philip believed and shared the Good News, and because he did others also came to believe.

A Sense of the Possible
Reflection Text
John 6:1-14

The feeding of the 5,000 is a familiar story. A great multitude of people had followed Jesus, and he was concerned about what they would eat. He turned to Philip and asked this question: "Where are we to buy bread for the people?" Why Philip? Some scholars have suggested that Philip was the disciple designated to care for the daily needs of the disciple band, that he was responsible for determining how much food to buy, when and where to buy it, how to ration and distribute it, and so on. If this was the case, it would be only natural for Jesus to turn to him with this question.

Others have suggested that since Jesus and the disciples may have been in the region of the Decapolis (an area of Greek cities) and Philip was from Bethsaida (a city that was close to some of these cities), he would have known best where and how to find food in the area.

Whatever the reason behind Jesus' question, Philip's response suggests that he must have already been calculating in his own mind how such a multitude could be fed. He knew that 200 denarii would buy only enough bread for each person to get a little. One denarius was equivalent to a day's wage for a common laborer. It would buy 36 small, flat barley biscuits about the size of a person's hand.

Philip had calculated that they could buy 7,200 of these biscuits, but that amount would not adequately feed the multitude of five-thousand-plus. Remember, the number 5,000 represented only the men present. Counting the women and children, the number would no doubt have been significantly higher. To make matters worse, Philip knew that many people baked only enough bread for their daily needs. To find so much bread on hand would be impossible, and no twenty-four-hour grocery stores were to be found. It looked like an impossible situation.

John tells his readers that Jesus knew all along what he would do about the situation. His question to Philip was a kind of test to see how Philip would respond. He had already seen Jesus turn water into wine and heal the sick, yet in his response to Jesus' question, Philip made no reference to the possibility that Jesus might hold the answer to the need at hand. He was a "facts-and-figures" person, too enamored with the facts of the situation to be open to the possibilities that faith introduces.

It has been said that the supreme essential for an effective statesman is "a sense of the possible." Philip approached this situation with a sense of the impossible. He had not yet learned that with God all things are possible (Matt 19:26). As the old chorus says, "Nothing is impossible when you put your trust in God!" Philip was learning a lesson of faith, a lesson that every disciple needs to learn. Whatever the circumstances, whatever the need, we may approach it with "a sense of the possible." With the apostle Paul we can say, "My God will fully satisfy every need . . . according to his riches in glory in Christ Jesus" (Phil 4:19).

A Vision of God
Reflection Texts
John 12:20-22; 14:8-11

The final days of Jesus' ministry had arrived. It was the time of the Passover, and Jesus and his disciples had come to Jerusalem. Some Greeks had also come to Jerusalem. These were probably Godfearers, or Gentiles who were attracted to Judaism but who had not converted, who had also come to Jerusalem for the Passover. They had heard about Jesus and wanted to meet this teacher who was the talk of the town. These Greeks came to Philip with a request: "Sir, we wish to see Jesus" (John 12:21). Why did they come to Philip? The fact that he had a Greek name may be one reason. The fact that John took the time to remind us that Philip was from Bethsaida may also be a clue since Bethsaida was heavily influenced by Greek ways. Perhaps they felt that this would make Philip open to their approach.

Up to this point, Jesus' ministry had been basically to Jews. Earlier, however, Jesus had indicated that he had come for the whole world. "For God so loved the world . . . " he had said, and in John 10:16 he had spoken of "other sheep that do not belong to this fold. I must bring them also, and they will listen to my voice." John 11:51-52 emphasizes this further: "Jesus was about to die for the nation, and not for the nation only, but to gather into one the dispersed children of God." Together with Andrew, Philip would have the privilege of sharing in bringing in the first of the great harvest from the nations of the world as he brought these Greeks to Jesus.

The request of these Greeks represents the world's request. The world is looking to the church, the community of present-day disciples of Jesus, to see Jesus. Do we, like Philip, bring the world to Jesus? Do others see Jesus in us? Consider this challenging question: If the world forms its opinion of Jesus from what it sees of Jesus in us, what kind of Jesus does the world see? The chorus of an old gospel song puts the challenge well:

> Let others see Jesus in you;
> Let others see Jesus in you;
> Keep telling the story,
> Be faithful and true,
> Let others see Jesus in you![5]

The request of the Greeks was somewhat similar to a request made by Philip as Jesus gathered with his disciples in the upper room on the night of his arrest (John 14:8-11): "Lord, show us the Father, and we will be satisfied." Jesus' response to Philip sets forth the central truth of the Christian message: "Whoever has seen me has seen the Father . . . I am in the Father and the Father is in me." In other words, if we want to see what God is like, we must look to Jesus!

In Jesus we meet God, the God who has come for us in Jesus to reconcile us to God's self. Since this is the case, the most pressing need in the life of any person is the need to see Jesus. In this Jesus we see the God who loves us, has redeemed us, and calls us. We must proclaim this Good News to our friends and to our world. There is a God who will meet every need, a God whose love extends to all people in every nation. We meet this God in Jesus. As Christians we have seen this God in Jesus Christ, and as his disciples we are called, like Philip, to invite others to "come and see."

Notes

[1] Tertullian, *Concerning Baptism*, 18.

[2] Eusebius, *Ecclesiastical History*, 3.31.2.

[3] See the apocryphal *Acts of Philip* for the tradition of his being crucified upside down in Hierapolis.

[4] William Paton, *The Church and the New Order* (Toronto: Macmillan, 1941) 152ff.

[5] B.B. McKinney, "Let Others See Jesus in You," 1924.

Simon the Zealot

Biblical Texts
Matthew 10:4; Mark 3:18; Luke 6:15; Acts 1:13

We have already learned that two disciples among the Twelve were called Judas. One Judas was, of course, notorious, the other almost forgotten. We have also discovered that two bore the name James. One of these was well known, while the other is all but forgotten. Did you know that there were also two disciples called Simon in the apostolic band? Of course everyone knows the Simon whom Jesus called Peter, the Rock. The other Simon, however, is, like the other Judas and the other James, all but forgotten.

Of course, the New Testament tells us very little about this Simon. Indeed, it tells us nothing whatsoever about him except his name, which appears in all four New Testament lists of the Twelve. Turn in your Bible to the lists of the Twelve found in Luke 6:15 and Acts 1:13. Do you find the name of Simon the Zealot? Now turn to the lists of the Twelve in Matthew 10:4 and Mark 3:18. Do you find the name of Simon the Zealot? When you compare the lists in Matthew and Mark with the lists in Luke and Acts, which name in Matthew and Mark is parallel to Simon the Zealot in Luke and Acts? If you answered Simon the Cananaean, you are absolutely right. But are these the same people? If they are, why the difference in names? The answer to this question lies in the meaning of the designation "Cananaean."

While some scholars have suggested that the designation "Cananaean" might mean that Simon was from Cana in Galilee or even that he might have been a Canaanite, such suggestions fail to deal adequately with the fact that the term Cananaean is derived from the Hebrew word *kana*, which means "jealous one." This term was used traditionally to describe someone who was jealous for the law of Israel. Indeed, a Cananaean was someone who was zealous for the law of Israel. Thus, Luke properly translated the term in his lists when he used the Greek word *zelotes*, which means "zealot." Simon the Cananaean and Simon the Zealot are two ways of saying the same thing, one reflecting the Hebrew and the other reflecting the Greek way of describing someone as a zealot.

As we have already noted, the New Testament tells us nothing about Simon. Apart from being a member of the apostolic band, he played no role in any scene in the New Testament. We only know that he was described as a zealot, but this in itself may tell us something very significant about Simon. While this may simply be a designation derived from the fact that Simon was zealous by nature, by the time the Gospels were written, the designation "zealot" had come to be attached to those persons who identified with a movement that Josephus called "the fourth philosophy" in first-century Judaism (the other three being the Sadduccees, Pharisees, and Essenes).

These people were fanatical Jewish nationalists who were zealous for the law of Israel and were bitter opponents of Roman rule. They were similar in many respects to the Pharisees, except for their passion for freedom and their refusal to call anyone master except God alone. They were eager to engage in a holy war that would lead to the overthrow of Roman domination and the reestablishment of Israel as an independent nation. They looked back to an earlier time when, under the leadership of the Hasmoneans (Judas the Maccabean and his brothers), Israel had thrown off the domination of the Syrian empire and existed as an independent nation, an independence that had lasted until the Romans took control of Palestine in 63 B.C.E.

Roman domination was never accepted by many Jews, some of whom believed that they should be responsible only to God and that God's commandments were the only ones to be obeyed. Thus, from the beginnings of Roman rule, Palestine was like a powder keg ready to explode at the slightest spark into violent revolt. With the death of Herod the Great, who had ruled as a Roman puppet king from 37 B.C.E. to 4 B.C.E., a group of nationalists stormed the palace at Sepphoris, raided the weapons arsenal, and incited just such a revolt. The insurrection was quickly put down by the Romans, and 2,000 of the insurrectionists were crucified!

A few years later the Romans installed a governor over Judea and Samaria who announced that a census would be taken for the purpose of taxation and administration. The idea of paying taxes of tribute to the Roman emperor seemed to many strict Jews to be nothing short of blasphemy. In their minds God was the only one worthy of tribute. Revolt broke out again under the leadership of Judas the Galilean. Once again the revolt was crushed, but while many died, the spirit of the revolt lived on. That spirit is captured in the following description of the Zealots from the pen of the first-century Jewish historian Josephus:

They have an inviolable attachment to liberty and say that God is their only Ruler and Lord. They do not mind dying any kind of death, nor do they heed the torture of their kindred and their friends, nor can any such fear make them call any man lord. And since this immovable resolution of theirs is known to a great many, I shall speak no further about that matter; for I am not afraid that anything that I have said about them will be disbelieved; but rather fear that what I have said comes short of the resolution they show when they undergo pain.[1]

Thus, the Zealots were fanatical Jewish nationalists who had a heroic disregard for the suffering involved in the struggle for what they regarded as the purity of their faith and life as a people. Theirs was an unquenchable zeal that would foster all kinds of terrorist and revolutionary activity throughout the first century, culminating in the Jewish revolt of 66 C.E. when Roman troops marched down from Syria, crushing Jewish resistance along the way until they finally surrounded and besieged Jerusalem. It was a hopeless situation for the Jews, many of whom starved to death inside the walls of the besieged city.

Finally in 70 C.E., the Romans destroyed Jerusalem and the temple, and the remaining Zealots and their sympathizers fled to a fortress south of Jerusalem by the Dead Sea called Masada. Here under the leadership of Eleazar they held out against the Romans for three more years. When it became clear that all hope of victory or escape was gone, Eleazar summoned the almost 1,000 people who remained there and made a stirring speech in which he urged them to slaughter their own wives and children and then to commit suicide rather than submit to the Romans.

Eleazar's speech captures the essence of the zealot spirit:

My loyal followers, long ago we resolved to serve neither the Romans nor anyone else but only God, . . . now the time has come that bids us prove our determination by our deeds. . . . hitherto we have never submitted to slavery; . . . we must not choose slavery now, and with it penalties which will mean the end of everything if we fall alive into the hands of the Romans. For we were first of all to revolt, and shall be the last to break off the struggle. And I think it is God who has given us this privilege, that we can die nobly and as free men, unlike others who were unexpectedly defeated. In our case it is evident that daybreak will end our resistance, but we are free to choose an honourable death with our loved ones. This our enemies cannot prevent, however earnestly they may pray to take us alive; nor can we defeat them in battle. . . . Not even the impregnability of our fortress has sufficed to save us, but though we have food in abundance, ample supplies of arms, and more than enough of every other requisite, God himself without a doubt has taken away all hope of survival . . . these things are God's vengeance for the many wrongs that in our madness we dared to do to our own countrymen.

For those wrongs let us pay the penalty not to our bitterest enemies, the Romans, but to God—by our own hands. It will be easier to bear. Let our wives die unabused, our children without knowledge of slavery; after that, let us do each other an ungrudging kindness, preserving our freedom as a glorious winding-sheet. But first let our possessions and the whole fortress go up in flames; it will be a bitter blow to the Romans, that I know, to find our persons beyond their reach and nothing left for them to loot. One thing only let us spare— our store of food; it will bear witness when we are dead to the fact that we perished, not through want but because, as we resolved at the beginning, we chose death rather than slavery.

According to Josephus, they took Eleazar at his word. "They tenderly embraced their wives, kissed their children, and began their bloody work. Two women and five children escaped by hiding in a cave."[2] When the Romans finally breached the walls of the fortress, they found 960 people dead.

If the designation attached to Simon's name indicates that he was in some way attached to this "zealot" movement, then he must have shared the convictions for which these Zealots eventually died. In fact, his own hopes to see the establishment of an independent Jewish kingdom possibly led him to Jesus in the first place. After all, many saw in Jesus the Messiah they had long anticipated, and if Jesus was the Messiah, then popular opinion held that he would be the one to lead the people to victory against the oppressive Romans. If Simon was a Zealot, then he becomes a powerful model of the way a life can be transformed by the power of Jesus Christ.

Discovering the Danger of Misguided Zeal

The Zealots were committed to a particular vision of what the Jewish nation should be and to the use of force to realize that vision. In fact, they were so convinced of the correctness of their vision that they gave no quarter to anyone with a different perception. When it became apparent that Jesus was not interested in leading in the violent overthrow of the Romans, he became of little consequence to most of those with zealot tendencies, and their commitment to their vision closed their minds to his vision of the Kingdom. In short, their zeal prevented them from being open to Jesus and his teaching. Oh, the danger of misguided zeal!

The tragedy of misguided zeal is also illustrated by the fact that, though the main concern of the Zealots was to wreak havoc against the Romans, at times they were willing to turn their swords against their own fellow Jews if they were perceived to be Roman collaborators. Nowhere is this seen more clearly than during the final days of the Jewish revolt that began in 66 C.E. With the Roman armies surrounding Jerusalem, Zealot leaders, each with his own vision of what should be done, began to turn on one another. Blinded by their zeal for their own way, even their fellow Jews came to be perceived as enemies!

Before the gavel of judgment falls too harshly upon these Zealots, however, we must remember that we are not immune from the pitfalls into which they fell. How many times have we been so blinded by our own understandings of scripture and our doctrinal preconceptions that we have allowed the truth of God to go unnoticed while pressing our own agendas to the bitter end? How often have we found ourselves making enemies out of fellow believers in our effort to see our own vision realized?

The harsh reality is that blind fanaticism not unlike that of the Zealots has too often plagued Christianity. The church has turned from a persecuted church to a persecuting church, resulting in the tortures of the Spanish Inquisition and the heresy trials of the Middle Ages. In fact, blind zeal caused the very people who came to America for freedom of worship and religion to instigate the heresy trials and witch hunts that darken the pages of our nation's early history. Zeal, even zeal for the truth, can become so reckless that it loses sight of that truth. Our zeal must always be tempered by a willingness to be responsive to truth whenever, wherever, and in whatever form it may come. Only God has a monopoly on the truth, and we must never be guilty of thinking that we have grasped all of that truth so well that we can sit in judgment on others.

Simon would not share in the tragic fate of the Zealot movement. Along the way he met Jesus of Nazareth. He heard him preaching and teaching about another kind of kingdom and another way of life by which that kingdom would be manifested. He was willing to hear of a different way, and whatever the cost, he was willing to follow.

Discovering a New Kind of Community

The fact that Simon had met Jesus and was open to what he said and did caused Simon's life to be transformed. He entered into a new relationship with God through Jesus Christ, which also brought about a transformation in his relationship to others. Because he was open to Jesus, he also came to be open to others. In fact, the disciple band represents a miracle in personal relationships.

Remember that Simon the Zealot was a member of the same disciple band that included Matthew the tax collector. As a tax collector, Matthew was a Roman collaborator. In other words, Matthew had worked for and with the very people who were hated by Zealots such as Simon. Someone has suggested that if the Zealot Simon and the tax collector Matthew had met under any other circumstances, Simon would probably have tried to kill Matthew! Instead, having met Jesus Christ, Simon the patriot and Matthew the traitor had come to live in peace with one another as part of the same fellowship.

Such a relationship demonstrates that no relationship exists that cannot be reconciled in and by the power of the love of Christ. This love binds people of the most diverse backgrounds into a new community in which they become one. It unites people with widely varying views and lifestyles and, therefore, becomes an incarnation in the world of the reconciling love of Christ.

As disciples we must ask ourselves if we are open to those who may be different from us—socially, racially, economically, politically, even religiously. Would people with as diverse views as those reflected by Simon and Matthew find room in our fellowship? What about those situations where we find ourselves disagreeing over doctrinal matters? Do we rush ahead in our zeal to exclude those with whom we disagree? Are we open to discovering the authenticity of their relationship to Christ and their commitment to Christ's lordship? Are we willing to allow our relationships to be controlled by the love of Christ?

The apostle Paul reflects on this idea in 2 Corinthians 5. He begins by reminding his readers (who were seriously divided among themselves) that the love of Christ must control their lives individually and corporately. Then he reminds them that they are no longer to judge one another according to human standards, but must see each other as God sees them, remembering that they are each one a part of the new creation in Jesus Christ. Recognizing that the Christ who is at work in us is also at work in the lives of others will help us to be open to share our lives with those who may be very different from us, as different as

Simon from Matthew. We too will become a model of the reconciling love of Jesus Christ fleshed out in the existence of a new community.

Discovering a New Kind of Life

The transformation that had taken place in Simon's life is also manifested in the fact that he is included in the list of the apostles found in Acts 1:13. In other words, Simon was still faithful to Jesus and the disciple band after the crucifixion and resurrection. He may have been attracted to Jesus because of his hope that Jesus would bring on the revolution that would lead to the establishing of the Kingdom. The Gospels suggest that many of the people who followed Jesus wanted to make him their earthly king, but when they realized that Jesus had another agenda, they turned their backs on him and looked elsewhere.

Simon did not turn his back on Jesus. He had come to understand that Jesus was the king and that he had come to establish a kingdom, but a very different kind of kingdom from what many people anticipated. He had come to understand the truth of Jesus' words that any kingdom that could be established by the sword could also be destroyed by the sword. Indeed, any kingdom set up by force is subject to defeat by a more powerful force, but a kingdom established on the basis of the permeating influence and power of love is a kingdom that no power can vanquish. It is a kingdom that can transcend all barriers —social, racial, economic, political, even religious.

Simon had come to understand that the struggle was no longer merely a struggle with the Romans, but a struggle with human sin, and that the object of the struggle was no longer merely freedom from the yoke of Roman bondage but from the bondage to human sin of which Roman oppression was a result. Simon discovered that this freedom is found in Christ and the new life he offers.

Jesus made it clear that the new life and power he offered could only come as the result of repentance—a giving up of the old life, a dying to self and those selfish goals that lead ultimately to our own destruction and the destruction of others. The way of Jesus' kingdom is not the way of the sword but the way of the cross. It requires dying to self that we might live to God. It manifests itself not in zealot-like force, but in sacrificial love that offers itself for others, even those who are perceived as enemies!

Simon was transformed from someone who was certain that he was right and determined to establish his kind of kingdom at any cost to someone who was willing to give himself as a suffering servant to the world even as his king had before him. No longer obsessed with wearing a crown, Simon was willing to take up a cross so that the transforming power of Christ's love that had made him a new person could be demonstrated for others to see.

A tradition about Simon recounted in *The Apostolic History of Abdias* (6.7-21) reflects the new man Simon the Zealot became. According to this tradition, Simon and Jude were preaching in Persia where they were opposed by two magicians, Zaroes and Arfaxat. The two magicians were outdone at every turn by Simon and Jude in demonstrations of wisdom and power. The king was so taken by Simon and Jude that he ordered them to kill the two magicians. They refused, however, saying, "Our God does not ask for forced service. If you will not believe, you may go free." The two magicians were freed, but they continued their opposition of Simon and Jude wherever they went.

In Suanir, a city with a great temple and seventy priests, they stirred up the people who brought Simon and Jude into their temple and offered them the choice of offering a sacrifice to their god or being put to death. At this point, an angel appeared to them and offered them a choice. Either they could escape and the temple and all the people would be destroyed, or they could suffer martyrdom. "Choose either the death of all here or the palm of martyrdom." They chose the palm of martyrdom, refusing to save their own lives by destroying the lives of others. They were subsequently attacked and killed.

Simon was willing to take up the cross and follow. Such a willingness must characterize the life of every disciple of Jesus. Two thousand years later Dietrich Bonhoeffer, who died in a Nazi concentration camp as a result of his efforts to follow Jesus, paraphrased Jesus' words in a powerful way: "When Christ calls a man, he bids him come and die."[3] That death includes death to our old life with all of the ideas that prevent us from being open to God's truth and other people. That death, demanded of every disciple in every age, delivers us from misguided zeal, a narrow exclusivism that shuts others out, and a life that substitutes our own self-centered striving for the way of the cross.

The question we must ask ourselves in this regard is nowhere more pointedly put than in the great old hymn that asks: " ' Are ye able,' said the Master, 'To be crucified with me?' " May the hymn writer's words be our response: " 'Yea,' the sturdy dreamers answered, 'To the death we follow thee!' "

Notes

[1]Josephus, *Antiquities of the Jews*, 18.1.6

[2]Josephus, *Jewish War*, 7,8,9.

[3]Dietrich Bonheoffer, *The Cost of Discipleship* (New York: Macmillan, 1963) 99.

James
Son of Zebedee

Biblical Texts
Mark 1:19-20; 3:13-17 par; 10:35-45;
Luke 9:51-56; Acts 12:1-2

Peter, James, and John appear to have formed a kind of inner circle among the twelve apostles. On several significant occasions (such as the raising of Jairus' daughter and the transfiguration experience), apparently these three disciples were the only disciples present. Of these three, James is probably the least well-known to most Christians.

With his father Zebedee, his mother Salome, and his brother John, James lived in or near Capernaum on the northern shore of the Sea of Galilee. There he and his father and brother were engaged in the family fishing business, and the fact that their father also employed "hired men" (Mark 1:20) suggests that their business was somewhat lucrative. Apparently, James' mother Salome was also a disciple of Jesus. Matthew 27:56 indicates that she followed Jesus and was present at the crucifixion.

In every list of the twelve apostles in the New Testament, James is found among the first three names. In Mark 3:17 and Acts 1:13 his name appears second only to that of Peter, while in Matthew 10:2 and Luke 6:14 it appears after the names of Peter and Andrew. The fact that his name always appears near the top of the list may suggest that he was seen as a leader in the apostolic band.

As with all of the apostles, there are a number of traditions about the life of James after the ascension of Jesus. *The Apostolic History of Abdias* (4.1-9) includes a story in which two magicians, Hermogenes and Philetus, are converted as a result of the ministry of James and go on to play an important role in another tradition, which explains why James is the patron saint of Spain. According to this tradition, James went to Spain where he had a significant ministry. Upon his return to Palestine, he was executed by Herod Agrippa I in 44 C.E. Hermogenes and Philetus set sail from the port of Joppa with his body. When they awoke the next morning, the ship on which they were sailing was off the coast of Spain. They landed at a place called Iria Flavia (known today as El Padron) where the body of James was laid and many miracles occurred. The body is said to be buried in Spain to this day.

As interesting as these traditions may be, we will focus our attention on three events in James' life as recorded in the New Testament from which we can learn significant truths about discipleship.

Zeal Tempered by Love
Reflection Text
Luke 9:51-56

Along with his brother John, James was given the nickname "Boanerges," which means "sons of thunder." The characteristic that may have given rise to this nickname is clearly seen in Luke 9:51-56. After an extended ministry in Galilee, the time had come for Jesus' final visit to Jerusalem. While many observant Jews would have taken a route that would have allowed them to bypass Samaria, Jesus had chosen to take the more direct ridge route that went straight south from Galilee to Judea through Samaria.

Luke tells us that Jesus sent messengers ahead to the Samaritan villages to prepare the way for his coming and arrange for food and lodging along the way. The messengers found that the Samaritans were reticent to receive Jesus. This should not surprise us, however, when we remember that there was no love lost between Jews and Samaritans. By the time of Jesus, the suspicious and hostile attitudes that existed between these two groups had been building for almost 500 years. Furthermore, the Samaritans were convinced that true worship was to be carried out on Mount Gerazim in Samaria rather than in Jerusalem's temple. The fact that Jesus had "set his face to go to Jerusalem" was just one more reason not to welcome him.

As we might expect, Jesus' disciples were angered by the unwillingness of the Samaritans to receive Jesus. Just how upset they were can be seen in the response of James and John to this situation: "Lord, do you want us to command fire to come down from heaven and consume them?" (Luke 9:54). Some texts add the words "as Elijah did" to the question, indicating that the disciples were alluding to the story in 2 Kings 1:9-16 in which Elijah called down fire from heaven to consume the representatives of Ahaziah.

The response of James and John is not a surprising one, but is it the kind of response that should characterize a disciple of Jesus? It was a response borne out of zeal for their master and his teachings, but it demonstrated a zeal without sensitivity. Notice Jesus' response. He turned and rebuked them. His mission, after all, was not to destroy but to save! It was a divine mission to a human race that had from its very inception refused to receive its true Lord. God was used to not being received. Yet God was willing to send His only Son to inhospitable humanity so that humanity might be saved. This is the magnificence of God's love and grace that has been manifested for all to see in Jesus Christ. We would not have responded to humanity's rebuff like that.

Martin Luther once suggested that if the world had treated him the way the world had treated God, he would have kicked it to pieces. That is the way we would respond; it is the way James and John responded. Jesus calls for another kind of response, however. He calls for a zeal with sensitivity to the love and grace of God that Jesus came to demonstrate and offer. He calls for a great missionary heart, and a great missionary heart is borne out of love rather than vindictive judgment—a love that keeps on loving even when one is rejected, a love in which the lover is willing to sacrifice self for the one who is loved!

The church is in desperate need of people who will love others enough to offer themselves for others. We are often all too ready to call down fire from heaven in judgment upon others. Then we must remember that it is by our love that people will know that we are Christians. Judgment, after all, is not ours to render, but love is ours to give! James and John had to learn this lesson, as should every disciple. Love is the theme of the disciple's life—a love for others that is prepared to die for others even when they reject that love. This is the way Jesus walked, and we who are his disciples are called to follow.

Faithful Servants
Reflection Text
Mark 10:35-45

Mark's Gospel records another incident that occurred on the journey to Jerusalem. James and John presented a request to Jesus: "Grant us to sit, one at your right hand and one at your left, in your glory" (10:37). As Galileans, James and John had grown up in the hotbed of Jewish nationalism. They believed that if Jesus was the Messiah, he would soon ascend the throne and establish his reign in Jerusalem. At long last, the messianic kingdom for which Jews had longed since the fall of Israel in 722 B.C.E. and the fall of Judah in 586 B.C.E. would become a reality. Their minds were enamored with the possibilities that such an eventuality offered.

As with any kingdom, there would be positions of prestige and power, and James and John saw themselves as likely candidates for those positions. After all, they had been with Jesus from the beginning. They had followed him every step of the way. So as they drew near to Jerusalem, they came with their request: the right hand and the left hand, the most privileged and powerful positions in the kingdom.

Two dimensions of discipleship stand out in this story. First, James and John revealed themselves to be men of great faith. As William Barclay observed, at the time of their request,

> nothing seemed less likely than that Jesus would ever sit on any throne. He was a homeless Galilean preacher, following a course which was bound to end in collision with the power of the authorities and in inevitable disaster; and yet even in that apparently hopeless situation James and John never doubted that Jesus Christ was a king.[1]

For such a faith that looks beyond the situation of the moment to an as yet unseen ultimate victory of God, James and John must be applauded. Regardless of the external circumstances, James and John believed that somehow Jesus would be king. Hebrews 11:1 describes faith as "the assurance of things hoped for, the conviction of things not seen." Disciples must be people of great faith who trust the God who holds the future and cling to the certainty of the accomplishing of God's purposes. Such faith enables the disciple to remain faithful whatever the circumstances may be.

A second dimension of discipleship also surfaces in this text. In this encounter with Jesus, James and John learned the true nature of the discipleship to which they had been called. The disciple of Jesus is called to be servant rather than master. Notice Jesus' teaching in response to their request for positions of privilege and power:

> So Jesus called them and said to them, "You know that among the Gentiles those whom they recognize as their rulers lord it over them, and their great ones are tyrants over them. But it is not so among you; but whoever wishes to become great among you must be your servant, and whoever wishes to be first among you must be slave of all. For the Son of Man came not to be served but to serve, and to give his life as a ransom for many." (Mark 10:42-45)

Jesus suggested that with their request James and John were thinking the way the world thinks. In the world where people lord it over one another and great men exercise authority, naturally we seek to sit in the seats of power and authority—the seats of great people. Jesus went on to say that this is not the way of the kingdom of God and, therefore, "it is not to be so among you."

The disciple of Jesus is called to be the servant of others. The words of Jesus suggest a shocking reversal of all that James and John had believed and experienced. They ran counter to their long-established views about the nature of the coming messianic kingdom. Their minds were captivated by possibilities of power. Jesus held before them an invitation to servanthood—to a lifestyle that he modeled before their eyes, the Son of Man who came "not to be served but to serve, and to give his life a ransom for many." This is the call of Jesus to his disciples in every age.

Faithful unto Death
Reflection Text
Acts 12:1-2

Acts 12:1-2 is the only text in the New Testament in which James appears apart from John. It presents the fulfillment of a word that Jesus had spoken to James and John in the incident on the way to Jerusalem recorded in Mark 10:34-39. In the course of his discussion of the nature of genuine discipleship, Jesus had asked James and John if they could drink "the cup" that he had to drink. The image of "the cup" appears again in Jesus' prayer in the Garden of Gethsemane where it clearly points to his impending death. The "cup" is the cup of obedience—obedience regardless of the outcome.

Jesus announced to James and John that the day would come when they would indeed drink the cup. Acts 12:1-2 tells how Jesus' words were fulfilled in the life of James. Luke describes how Herod Agrippa I, the grandson of Herod the Great, "laid violent hands upon some who belonged to the church. He had James, the brother of John, killed with the sword." In this way James became the first of the apostles to be martyred for his faith. He was faithful, even unto death.

Note that "when he [Herod] saw that it [the murder of James] pleased the Jews, he proceeded to arrest Peter also" (Acts 12:3). This raises an interesting question. Apparently, when Herod decided to lay hands upon some persons who belonged to the church, James was the primary target. There may be many reasons for this, of course, but this verse is suggestive of the possibility that James was still "thundering" and as a result of the power and prominence of his witness was clearly recognized as the obvious target. In other words, James stood out above all the rest, and when the storm breaks, lightning strikes the tallest tree! Peter was put in jail, but James was put to death! Did Herod see James as the bigger threat? Did he feel that James' "thundering" had to be stopped? Whatever the reasons, when the time of testing came, James remained faithful, even unto death.

Thus, while we have few recorded words from the lips of James, his life speaks volumes as a model of the kind of faith and faithfulness that should characterize the disciple of Jesus. James was willing to count the cost of discipleship and pay the price, whatever the price might be. He had a faith that looked beyond the present circumstances to the ultimate victory of the purposes of God and a willingness to serve even to the point of sacrificing himself so that others might come to know the Savior.

According to early Christian tradition, the faith and faithfulness of James at the time of his execution inspired others to announce their faith in Christ. Eusebius relates the story that he found in the seventh book of the lost *Hypotyposes* of Clement of Alexandria in which Clement describes how the one who led James to court was so moved by his testimony that he confessed that he was also a Christian. Subsequently, both were both led away to be executed, and both beheaded at the same time. On the way to their deaths, James' former captor begged James to forgive him, "and James looked at him for a moment and said, 'Peace be to you' and kissed him."[2]

James thundered across the land and made a difference for countless numbers of people who came to faith in Christ because of his faithful witness. How is it with us? Are we thundering forth the gospel? Perhaps we might put the question another way. Today, if people were arrested for being a Christian, would there be enough evidence to convict you? It is time to join with James on the journey with Jesus and count the cost of discipleship!

Notes

[1]William Barclay, *The Master's Men* (London: SCM, 1959) 100-101.
[2]Eusebius, *Ecclesiastical History* 2.9.2-3.

John

Biblical Texts
Mark 9:38-41; Mark 10:35-41; Luke 9:51-56

While we know very little about some of Jesus' first disciples, the New Testament and early Christian tradition give much attention to the apostle John. According to this tradition, John is to be identified with the disciple whom Jesus loved in the Fourth Gospel and is held to be the author of five New Testament books: the Gospel of John, the Epistles of John, and the Apocalypse of John. From New Testament references to John we not only learn of the things that he did but also something of the kind of person he must have been. Let us begin our look at this "beloved disciple" by summarizing what the New Testament tells us about him. Then we will turn our attention to three incidents in the ministry of Jesus in which John played a major role to see what we can learn about discipleship.

With his father Zebedee, his mother Salome, and his brother James, John lived in or near Capernaum on the northern shore of the Sea of Galilee. There he worked with his father, his brother, and the "hired men" (Mark 1:20, suggesting that they were somewhat well-to-do) in the family fishing business. Luke 5:10 suggests that they may also have been involved in a partnership with Simon Peter and Andrew. According to the Gospel accounts, while James and John were in their boat mending their nets Jesus called them to follow him (see Mark 1:16-20).

Have you ever noticed how much more natural it is to say "James and John" rather than "John and James"? The fact is, of course, that whenever these two are mentioned together in the New Testament, James is always mentioned first, and while we cannot know this for sure, it probably indicates that James was the older of the two brothers. Some scholars have even suggested that James and John were actually related to Jesus. This view is based on an examination of the three lists of the women who were at the cross.

In Mark 15:40 the women at the cross are listed as Mary Magdalene, Mary the mother of James the less and Joses, and Salome. In John 19:25 they are Jesus' mother, his mother's sister, Mary the wife of Clophas, and Mary Magdalene. In Matthew 27:56 they are Mary

Magdalene, Mary the mother of James and Joses, and the mother of Zebedee's children. Mary Magdalene is found in all three lists. Mary the mother of James and Joses and Mary the wife of Clophas may be identified as the same person. Thus, the remaining person is called Salome in Mark, the sister of Jesus' mother in John, and the mother of Zebedee's children in Matthew. If all three references are to the same person, then Salome—the mother of Zebedee's children—was also the sister of Jesus' mother, and James and John were cousins of Jesus.

Matthew, Mark, and Luke all agree Peter, James, and John formed something of an inner circle among the Twelve. These three alone were with Jesus on several significant occasions including the raising of Jairus' daughter (Mark 5:35-43), the transfiguration (9:2-8), and the Garden of Gethsemane (14:32-42). If the ancient tradition identifying John with the disciple "whom Jesus loved" in the Fourth Gospel is correct, then the Gospel of John sheds further light on John. At the Last Supper, this disciple appears "reclining next to him" (John 13:21-25). He is later found standing at the foot of the cross where Jesus committed his mother to his continuing care (19:26-27). In John 20:2-10 it is the "beloved disciple" who arrives first at the empty tomb and sees and believes. Later by the Sea of Galilee he is the first to recognize the risen Jesus (21:7).

When Jesus and his disciples went to Jerusalem for the last time to celebrate the Passover, Jesus sent John and Peter ahead to prepare the place for the meal (Luke 22:8). After Jesus' death and resurrection, we find John and Peter together in several stories in the book of Acts. As a result of the healing of a lame beggar, he and Peter were arrested and stood before the Sanhedrin where they were charged to preach and teach no more in the name of Jesus (Acts 3–4). Later John was sent with Peter to Samaria to investigate the conversion of the Samaritans and to nurture the new converts there (Acts 8). It is not surprising that Paul described John as one of the "pillars" of the church in Jerusalem (Gal 2:9). Clearly he continued to have a significant ministry in and around Jerusalem after Jesus' death.

Looking beyond the Acts account there are conflicting traditions about the life of John.[1] One tradition says that he was martyred at the same time that his brother James was put to death. The death of James is alluded to in Acts 12:1-2 and occurred in the year 44. The most widespread tradition, however, says that he remained in Jerusalem for a period of time and then went to the city of Ephesus where he lived to an old age and died a natural death.[2] During his ministry there he is said to have raised a man from the dead and opposed the heretic Cerinthus, who taught that Jesus never had a body of flesh and blood but was only a phantom with the appearance of a man. During the reign of the Roman emperor Domitian, John was banished to the Isle of Patmos but released by Domitian's successor Nerva and allowed to return to Ephesus where he lived until the time of the emperor Trajan who ruled from 98 to 117.[3]

In his *Commentary on Galatians* Jerome says that John died in the sixty-eighth year after the Lords's death, having founded and built churches throughout Asia Minor. He recounts the following incident from John's final years:

> When John tarried in Ephesus to extreme old age, and could only with difficulty be carried to the church in the arms of his disciples, and was unable to give utterance to many words, he used to say no more at their several meetings than this, "Little children, love one another." At length the disciples and fathers who were there, wearied with always hearing the same words, said: "Master, why dost thou always say this?" "It is the Lord's command," was his reply, "and if this alone be done, it is enough."[4]

Three important incidents in John's life help us to understand more about John and set significant truths about the nature of discipleship.

To Save, Not to Destroy
The Danger of Intolerance
Reflection Text
Luke 9:51-56

Jesus and his disciples were on their way from Galilee to Jerusalem. The most direct route took them through Samaria. Of course, many strict Jews would never take this route. Instead, they would go around Samaria by crossing the Jordan River to the east and traveling down its eastern shore until they were opposite Jericho. Here they would recross the Jordan and travel through Jericho up to Jerusalem. Jesus, however, had chosen to take the more direct route through Samaria. This provided him with an opportunity to teach John and the other disciples an important truth. According to the Lukan account, Jesus had sent messengers ahead to make arrangements for food and lodging in a Samaritan village. The messengers returned to report that the Samaritans would not receive him.

The reaction of Jesus' disciples was one of anger and contempt. It was, in fact, a very normal reaction. Feeling slighted and insulted, they were ready to reek vengeance on the Samaritans. At this point John and his brother James came to Jesus with a suggestion in the form of a question: "Lord, do you want us to command fire to come down from heaven and consume them?" (Luke 9:55). This question is not surprising, is it? It reflects the typical human reaction to those we perceive to be enemies, no matter who they are.

Notice Jesus' response to the question from John and James: he rebuked them! Then, according to many ancient texts, he reminded them that the Son of Man came not to destroy people's lives but to save them. Who are these people that Jesus came to save? All people—Jews to be sure, but also Samaritans! The Son of Man came to save all people, for all people are guilty of refusing to receive God and make God's purposes their own. All people are in rebellion against God.

What is God's response to humanity's rebellion? Has he sent fire from heaven to destroy us? No! In Romans 5:8 Paul reminds us that "while we were still sinners (that is, while we were engaged in active rebellion against God) Christ died for us!" This is the Good News. This is the gospel. Christ has come not to destroy us but to save us, all of us, and if this is God's purpose for humankind, it must be our purpose too. Of course this will mean a new way of relating to others, even those we perceive to be our enemies.

On the road to Jerusalem that day, John was a long way from being the disciple who more than any other would focus on Jesus' teaching about God's love for us and our love for one another. He was still blinded by the normal human tendency to strike out at others rather than to lay down our lives for others, but he was learning. Years later he wrote these words that demonstrate he had learned the lesson well:

> Beloved, let us love one another, because love is from God; everyone who loves is born of God and knows God. Whoever does not love does not know God, for God is love. God's love was revealed among us in this way: God sent his only Son into the world so that we might live through him. In this is love, not that we loved God but that he loved us and sent his Son to be the atoning sacrifice for our sins. Beloved, since God loved us so much, we also ought to love one another. (1 John 4:7-12)

The "Us/Them" Syndrome
The Danger of Exclusivism
Reflection Text
Mark 9:38-41

John appears alone in only one narrative in the New Testament. Jesus and his disciples were on their final journey to Jerusalem. All along the way Jesus had been teaching them very important lessons about the meaning of discipleship. In fact, by the time Jesus and the disciples reached the point on their journey described in our reflection text, Jesus had twice spoken of his own impending suffering and death (Mark 8:31; 9:30-32) and twice emphasized that those who are his disciples must be willing to deny themselves, take up their own crosses, and follow him (8:34-38; 9:35-37). In other words, Jesus clearly sets before those who would be his disciples the conditions of discipleship: a disciple of Jesus must be willing to put Christ and others first, and must be the servant of all (9:35)!

We can see the pattern of Jesus' teaching very clearly in the verses leading up to our reflection text. Notice the structure of the biblical narrative. Be sure to read each text.

9:30-32   Jesus foretells his own suffering and death.

9:33-34   The disciples seem to misunderstand Jesus, for while he is talking about suffering and death, they are discussing positions of prestige and power in the kingdom! There is little room in their thinking for any notion of suffering service.

9:35-37   Jesus tries to redirect their thinking. Rather than focusing their attention on prestige and power, they should be thinking about the nature of servanthood—a servanthood in which even children are to be served (a very unacceptable notion in first-century society in which children were seen as having very little value).

The call of Jesus is clear. All who would be his disciples must be willing to be the servants of others—all others—even children! Against this backdrop, the story in verses 38-41 becomes especially significant. Stop for a moment and read the text carefully.

How would you characterize John's attitude toward the unnamed man who was casting out demons in Jesus' name? It seems pretty clear, doesn't it? Notice the justification he offers. "We tried to stop him, because he was not following us" (9:38). Was John willing to be a servant to this man? Apparently not. Instead, he wanted to "lord it over him" (10:42). But there is more. John's hostile attitude toward the man appears to be rooted in the fact that "he was not following us." In effect he was saying, "He is not one of us. He does not belong to our group. He doesn't always go where we go or do what we do. He's not like us. He doesn't look the same, dress the same, or speak the same. He doesn't dots all of his 'i's' like we do, nor does he cross his 't's' like we do, and until he gets in step with the rest of us, we have no place for him!"

John's reaction represents the kind of narrow exclusivism that has resulted in tragic consequences throughout the history of the church. It is a kind of exclusivism in which we set ourselves up as the arbiters of truth. We become judge and jury over others. Such an attitude is often displayed toward those outside of the church, and it is all too often displayed toward brothers and sisters within the church.

The New Testament is full of examples. According to 1 Corinthians 1:10-13, for example, the Corinthian church was being pulled apart by groups, each claiming to be right, each one sure that it held the keys to genuine orthodoxy. Paul wrote a scathing letter to this congregation reminding them that the heart of the gospel is the ministry of reconciliation. In other words, as he put it in 1 Corinthians 13, even if we dot all the "i's" and cross all the "t's" correctly, but do not relate to one another in love, we are nothing!

In Philippians, Paul addresses another situation where disunity prevailed because people were not willing to be servants to one another. Instead they had set themselves up over against one another. Listen to his exhortation:

> Do nothing from selfish ambition or empty conceit, but in humility regard another as better than yourselves. Let each of you look not to your own interests, but to the interests of others. (2:3-4)

Paul suggested the solution to their problem in verses 5-8:

> Let the same mind be in you that was in Christ Jesus, who, though he was in the form of God, did not regard equality with God as something to be exploited, but emptied himself, taking the form of a slave and being born in human likeness. And being found in human form, he humbled himself and became obedient to the point of death—even death on a cross.

John was plagued by an attitude of narrow exclusivism, but he was not the only one to succumb to this temptation. Individual Christians, local congregations, and denominations have all too easily fallen into this trap for 2,000 years. Jesus' response to John is his response to all of us who would fall into that trap. He rebuked John for his narrow exclusivism. He reminded him that God is free to be at work when and where and in whomever God chooses. Our task, the disciple's task, is not to sit in judgment. Our task is to serve and be open to the way(s) God is at work around us—even ways that may strike us as quite unusual and different from our own for "whoever is not against us is for us" (Mark 9:40).

Self-Serving Ambition or Self-Less Sacrifice
Reflection Text
Mark 10:35-41

The journey toward Jerusalem and the cross continued. Jesus spoke again of his suffering and death (Mark 10:32-34). Three times he had spoken of his fate. Twice he had followed this teaching by announcing that all who would be his disciples must follow him in suffering service toward others. John appeared again, this time once again with his brother James. They had a request to put to Jesus. "Teacher, we want you to do for us whatever we ask of you" (v. 35).

Now think of the implications of this request. Jesus, obedient to God's will for his life, was marching toward Jerusalem and the cross where he would offer himself not only for John and his brother James, but for all humanity. He had called his disciples to follow after him—to follow him on the way to the cross. This is his call to disciples in every age. The only question concerns the nature of our response.

How did John and James respond to that call? Somehow in spite of all that Jesus had said to them about the nature of discipleship, they had not yet really understood his call. In spite of his repeated emphasis on serving others, their attention was still focused on themselves. Their concern was with what Jesus could do for them. Notice their specific request in verse 37: "Grant us to sit, one at your right hand and one at your left, in your glory." Their eyes were focused on the glories of the kingdom that they believed Jesus would soon set up in Jerusalem. Their concern was that they would have the most powerful places in that kingdom. They wanted to be the Secretary of State and the Secretary of Defense in the king's cabinet! Their request grew out of self-serving ambition.

In his response, Jesus sought to focus their thinking in another and very different direction:

> You know that among the Gentiles those whom they recognize as their rulers lord it over them, and their great ones are tyrants over them. But it is not so among you, but whoever wishes to become great among you must be your servant, and whoever wishes to be first among you must be slave of all. (vv. 42-44)

The concern of John and James was a concern for self. It was the same kind of self-serving ambition that led to humanity's fall, and such self-centeredness lies at the heart of human sin. Jesus' concern, on the other hand, is concern for others, and just such a selfless concern lies at the heart of genuine discipleship.

Like John and James, we are committed to being disciples of Jesus, but is it possible that we too have not really understood his call? Is our response to Jesus based on what we want Jesus to do for us? Is our commitment to self-aggrandizement or to the advancement of the Kingdom? On the journey to Jerusalem, John was beginning to learn what every disciple in every age must learn. The way of the disciple is the way of the master who has gone before. The way of Jesus is summed up in his own words in verse 45: "For the Son of Man came not to be served but to serve, and to give his life a ransom for many." It would not be long before John would come to understand what Jesus meant. It would not be long before Calvary.

From the life of John we can learn much about the nature of genuine discipleship. It grows from a commitment to save rather than to destroy. It manifests itself in a commitment to serve others that leaves no place for narrow exclusivism and self-serving ambition. John learned these lessons well. May it also be so for you and me!

Notes

[1]For a careful examination of the many traditions about John, see R. Alan Culpepper, *John, The Son of Zebedee: The Life of a Legend* (Columbia SC: University of South Carolina Press, 1993).

[2]According to Nicephorus (*The Ecclesiastical History*, 2.2), John stayed in Jerusalem caring for Jesus' mother until the day of her death.

[3]See, for example, Irenaeus, *Against Heresies*, 5.30.3; Eusebius, *Ecclesiastical History*, 3.18.1; Jerome, *On Illustrious Men*, 9.

[4]Jerome, *Commentary on the Epistle to the Galatians*, 6.10.

Matthew

Biblical Texts
Matthew 9:9-13; 10:3;
Mark 2:13-17; 3:18; Luke 5:27-32; 6:15

"Hey! Wait a minute," you may be saying. "I thought our study was about Matthew. Why is our reflection text about Levi?" Your question is well-taken and points to an important consideration with which we must begin our study of this disciple. When one compares the three passages that tell the story of the call of Matthew, something interesting emerges. Consider these texts:

> As Jesus was walking along, he saw a man called Matthew sitting at the tax booth; and he said to him, "Follow me." And he got up and followed him. (Matt 9:9)

> As he was walking along, he saw Levi son of Alphaeus sitting at the tax booth, and he said to him, "Follow me." And he got up and followed him. (Mark 2:14)

> After this, he went out and saw a tax collector named Levi sitting at the tax booth; and he said to him, "Follow me." And he got up, left everything, and followed him. (Luke 5:27-28)

An examination of these texts suggests that, as was often the case in first-century Palestine, Matthew had two names. His given name was probably Levi, a good Jewish name that may indicate his family was of the priestly tribe of Levi or was at least sympathetic to the concerns and ideals of that tribe. Matthew is usually taken to mean "gift of God," but two other possibilities should be considered.

Some biblical researchers have suggested that Matthew comes from an Aramaic word meaning "manly," and thus may represent an epithet given to reflect an element of his character. Others have argued that Matthew is Greek for the Hebrew *Mathya* or *Mattai*, an abridged form of *Mattathiah* or *Mattathias*. The name *Mattathias* was as familiar to first-century Jews as the name Patrick Henry is to twentieth-century Americans, for he was a great national hero to the Jews.

In the 160s B.C.E. when the Jews were under the domination of the Seleucid (Syrian) empire, an aged priest named Mattathias had slain a Seleucid military officer who had come to force him and the people of his village to perform a pagan sacrifice. His act triggered a Jewish revolt that led to the establishment of an independent Jewish kingdom that lasted until 63 B.C.E. Perhaps the name Matthew had been given to Levi because, like Mattathias of old, he had come to demonstrate a zeal for God. In this case, it would be an epithet similar to the one Jesus gave to Simon when he called him "Peter." In Peter's case the epithet stuck; maybe the same thing happened to Levi.

The Markan account of the call of Levi suggests another interesting possibility with regard to this disciple. Notice that Mark refers to him as "son of Alphaeus." According to the lists of the Twelve in Matthew 10:3, Mark 3:18, Luke 6:15, and Acts 1:13, there was another member of the apostolic band who was a son of Alphaeus: James. If this Alphaeus is the same person, then Matthew and this James were brothers, which would mean that there were three sets of brothers among the Twelve: Peter and Andrew; James and John; and Matthew and James, the sons of Alphaeus.

While the New Testament contains only one story about Matthew, there are many traditions about his life after the ascension of Jesus. According to some traditions, he first preached to his own people in Judea and was later allotted the territory of Ethiopia as his mission. Other traditions associate him with Persia, Parthia, and Macedonia. Most interesting is the tradition that Matthew wrote a gospel in Hebrew. According to Irenaeus,

> Now Matthew published among the Hebrews a written gospel also in their own tongue, while Peter and Paul were preaching in Rome and founding the Church.[1]

Similarly, Jerome wrote:

> Matthew who is also called Levi, and who changed from a tax-gatherer into an apostle, was the first one in Judea to write a gospel of Jesus Christ in Hebrew letters and words for those of the circumcision who believed; but who translated it afterwards into Greek is not sufficiently certain.[2]

The earliest testimony comes from Papias who said: "Matthew collected the oracles [of the Lord] in the Hebrew language, and each interpreted them as best he could."[3] This description suggests that Matthew's Hebrew Gospel was a collection of the sayings of Jesus that may have later been incorporated into our present Gospel of Matthew.

The one story in the New Testament about Matthew tells us that he was a tax collector. Some translations refer to tax collectors as publicans. Essentially these two words mean the same thing. The term "publican" comes from the Latin word *publicanus,* which was used of persons who were engaged in public service, especially those who handled public money such as tax collectors. Tax collectors were among the most despised and hated classes of people in the ancient world. In fact, according to Cicero, tax collectors and usurers were the two most despised and hated trades.[4]

Nowhere was the hatred of tax collectors more pronounced than among the Jews of Palestine. In the Roman system, the collection of taxes was farmed out to locals. Basically, the job was sold to the highest bidder, and since the job could be quite lucrative, the bidding often went very high. Since the Romans paid no salaries to the tax collectors, they were allowed to charge as much over the legal levy as they could get. Anything over and above the required levy, they could keep for themselves. Thus, their income was based on overtaxing their neighbors! Furthermore, they had the authority of the Roman government in the form of the Roman army to ensure that taxes were paid. If necessary, they could take away a man's house, imprison his family, or impound his beast of burden. One can see how such a system would not contribute to the popularity of tax collectors, who were considered little better than thieves or extortioners.

Tax collectors were also considered to be traitors by those Jews who considered God alone to be worthy to receive tribute. To pay tribute to Caesar was to infringe upon the prerogatives of the God of Israel. Since the Romans farmed out the collection of this tribute to locals such as Matthew, the tax collectors were Jews who were seen as having turned against their own people and against God. It is little wonder that they were classed with murderers, harlots, and sinners. They were banned from public worship, unacceptable as witnesses in court, and unable to be judges.

Matthew appears to have belonged to a category of tax collectors known as *Mohkes,* a kind of customs officer. The following description of these customs officers is instructive:

> There were great numbers of these customs officers, for government practice was to make one man responsible in one place for the collection of one particular kind of tax or duty, and such taxes and duties were legion. There was an import and an export tax, which was a main source of government revenue. That tax might be

anything from two-and-a-half to twelve-and-a-half percent on the value of goods imported or exported; or it might be worked on a tariff system on certain articles, as it was in Syria. There was a purchase tax on all that was bought and sold. There was bridge money to be paid when a bridge was crossed; road money to be paid when main roads were used; harbor duty to be paid when a harbor was entered; market money to be paid when a market was used; town dues to be paid when a traveler entered a walled town. If a man was traveling on a road, he might have to pay a tax for using the roads, a tax on his cart, on its wheels, on its axle and on the beast which drew the cart. There was a tax on crossing rivers, on ships, on the use of harbor quays, on dams; there were certain licenses which had to be paid for engaging in certain trades. The Roman peace, the Roman roads, the Roman civil service, the Roman good order and government cost money to run, and the government was fertile in discovering different kinds of taxes to enable it to pay its way.[5]

Matthew functioned as a part of this system, and his post in or near Capernaum sat on the great highway that ran from Damascus to the Mediterranean seaport of Acre—a strategic and lucrative location indeed! Here he met Jesus.

The Call of Matthew
Reflection Text
Luke 5:26

According to Matthew, Mark, and Luke, Jesus made Capernaum something of a headquarters during his Galilean ministry. Thus, he was in and out of the town frequently, and likely Matthew had known of and, perhaps, even had some contact with Jesus prior to his call. There can be little doubt that Peter, Andrew, James, and John knew Matthew in his role as tax collector. Imagine the looks of astonishment that must have marked their faces when Jesus stopped in front of the tax office and called to Matthew with the invitation to "Follow me!"

Surely the disciples must have thought the Master had made a mistake. Matthew was, after all, a tax collector! But Jesus had made no mistake. In fact, his invitation to Matthew was something of an acted parable. It announced to all with eyes to see and ears to hear that the love of God embraces all and that the grace of God extends to all. This "amazing grace" was for Peter and Andrew, James and John, *and* Matthew the tax collector.

Look at the list of the twelve apostles in Matthew 10:1-4. Do you notice anything interesting about the way Matthew is listed? Matthew is the only disciple whose occupation is given along with his name in the list of the twelve apostles. Is this accidental? I think not. For the early Christians, the fact that Matthew the tax collector was invited to join the apostolic band was an announcement that Jesus' call is for "whosoever will." This is good news! No matter how far short of the glory of God a person may have fallen, God's grace is sufficient. God's grace *is* greater than all our sin. The call of Matthew is a concrete demonstration of this grace. As one writer put it,

> a crucial eccentricity of the Christian faith is the assertion that people are saved by grace. There's nothing *you* have to do. There's nothing you *have* to do. There's nothing you have *to do*. . . . Grace is something you can never get but only be given. There's no way to earn it or deserve it or bring it about any more than you can deserve the taste of raspberries and cream or earn good looks or bring about your own birth. . . . There's only one catch. Like any other gift, the gift of grace can be yours only if you'll reach out and take it.[6]

Jesus offered Matthew the grace of God that day. He reached out and took it. His response must have been as shocking to the disciples as Jesus' offer!

Matthew's Response
Reflection Text
Luke 5:28

Jesus' call to Matthew was simple and direct. It was the same call heard by Peter and Andrew, James and John, and Philip. It contains within it the essence of discipleship: to be a disciple of Jesus is to follow Jesus. Matthew's response was also simple and direct. Matthew "left everything, and followed him," which required a radical decision to turn his back on his past and his profession. True, the other disciples had left their fishing nets to follow Jesus, but if things did not work out with Jesus, they could always go back to fishing. Matthew, however, would have nothing to fall back on.

He would not be able to return to his job. He would never be trusted with the tax money after this. After all, he had just up and walked off, leaving the office and the monies at the mercy of whoever happened by. Furthermore, there would have been a long line of people ready to take his place, and who in the community would ever hire him after the way he had treated them as tax collector! When Matthew walked out of that tax office, he was taking a significant risk. He was trusting his future to an itinerant Galilean rabbi. He had burned his bridges behind him.

Clearly, Matthew models the kind of obedience to Jesus' call that should characterize every disciple. Matthew was willing to go wherever Jesus led, whatever the cost might be. Is this the kind of obedience that marks our lives? What would happen if we had to leave our jobs to be faithful to Jesus? And what of those other things in our lives that we cling to for our security rather than trusting Jesus as our security? Matthew "left everything" to follow Jesus. Have we?

Luke goes on to tell us in 5:29 that Matthew "gave a great banquet . . . in his house." One can sense the joy and enthusiasm of Matthew for his new faith. The discovery of Jesus and the new life he offers naturally leads to celebration. We should not be surprised that one of Jesus' favorite analogies for the kingdom of God was a wedding feast—a time of joy and celebration. As with others who found Jesus, Matthew wanted to share his discovery and joy with others, so he invited "a large crowd of tax collectors" to gather at his table. Obviously, these were Matthew's friends. He wanted to share his new-found treasure with his friends. Once again, as in the cases of Philip and Andrew, the pattern for disciples is clear. Those who find Jesus want to share Jesus with others. If one test of the measure of our Christianity is how much we want to share it with others, Matthew passed that test with flying colors!

Someone has said, "Evangelism . . . is one beggar telling another beggar where to get food."[7] The world is starving for the food that only God can provide. Indeed, what the world needs most is to know that God's love and mercy are available, that "whosoever will may come" and receive them. Yet, we must also consider the person next door or three houses down in our neighborhood, the person in the office next door or at the desk next to mine. These are the people who need an invitation to the banquet. Like Matthew, we have heard Jesus' invitation and taken our seat. Now let us invite our friends, our communities, our world to join us at the gospel feast!

Notes

[1]Irenaeus, *Adv. Haer.* 3.1.1, cited by Eusebius, *Ecclesiastical History*, 5.8.2.

[2]Jerome, *Concerning Illustrious Men*, 3.

[3]Quoted by Eusebius in his *Ecclesiastical History*, 3.39.16.

[4]Cicero, *De Officiis*, 1.42.

[5]William Barclay, *The Master's Men* (London: SCM, 1959) 59-60.

[6]Frederick Buechner, *Wishful Thinking* (New York: Harper & Row, 1973) 33-34.

[7]This well-known saying is attributed to D. T. Niles.

James
Son of Alphaeus

Biblical Texts
Matthew 10:3; Mark 3:18; Luke 6:15; Acts 1:13

Every church has a host of unsung heroes, those "unsung saints" who faithfully carry out their roles and responsibilities but get very little notice in the press. In many ways, these "forgotten followers" are the very backbone of the church without whom its ministries would quickly come to a screeching halt. They are the salt of the earth, though they may never make the headlines.

James, the son of Alphaeus, may well represent these "unsung saints." Certainly he is overshadowed by the other two James of the New Testament: James, the son of Zebedee, who along with Peter and his brother John made up a kind of inner circle among the apostles; and James, the brother of Jesus, who came to be the leader of the Jerusalem church.

The New Testament tells us nothing about this James except his name, which appears at the same point in every New Testament list of the Twelve (Matt 10:3; Mark 3:18; Luke 6:15; Acts 1:13). The fact that he is described as the son of Alphaeus is suggestive, however, of an interesting possibility that is not directly mentioned in the New Testament. Compare the call of Matthew (Matt 9:9) and Levi (Mark 2:14). If, as many people believe, Matthew and Levi are, in fact, the same person, then Mark tells us that Matthew was also a son of Alphaeus! Could Matthew and James possibly have been brothers? This has been the conclusion of some persons, though the two disciples are never referred to as brothers in the New Testament itself.

Note that James heads the list of the third group of four disciples in each of the New Testament lists of the Twelve. Look at these lists in Matthew 10:3-4, Mark 3:16-19, Luke 6:14-16, and Acts 1:13, and notice the group of four names beginning with James, the son of Alphaeus. Perhaps the fact that these four are consistently mentioned together may indicate that they shared some kind of common bond.

Notice the other three names. Simon is called "the Zealot," which could indicate that he had been involved with the radical movement of

Jewish nationalists who sought to overthrow the existing Roman governance of Palestine. Then there is Judas Iscariot. Many persons have argued that he was at least sympathetic to the Zealot movement if not, in fact, a Zealot himself. Finally, there is Thaddeus in Matthew and Mark, and Judas the son of James in Luke and Acts. Very likely these are two names for the same person. Nevertheless, Thaddeus is also referred to as a Zealot in several manuscripts of the *Apostolic Constitutions*, and Judas the son of James is referred to as Judas the Zealot in one important Latin manuscript.[1] Could these four possibly have been bound together by their deep commitment to Jewish nationalism? While we cannot be sure, the evidence is at least suggestive that this may have been the case. If so, it tells us a little more about this James.

One further possible piece of information may be drawn from Mark 15:40, in which Mark names the women who were at the cross. He mentions a Mary who was the mother of James "the *mikros*" and Joses. If this is the same James, then we may know several other things about him. The designation *mikros* is most likely a reference to either the fact that James was small in stature (James, "the small one") or to his age (James, "the young one"). In either case it was a nickname given to distinguish this James—either by means of physical appearance or age—from some other James who would be known to Mark's readers, perhaps James, the son of Zebedee or James, the brother of Jesus. Furthermore, if this is the same James, then we know that other members of his family (at least his mother who was at the cross) were followers of Jesus.

Faithful without Fanfare

Unlike many of the disciples of Jesus, very little attention is given to James in early Christian tradition. One tradition says that he preached in Southwest Palestine and Egypt and was martyred by crucifixion in Ostrakine in Egypt.[2] Another tradition tells of his preaching in Persia.[3] No wonder this apostle is often called "James the Less"—we certainly know less about him than most of the others.

Yet, the fact that his name appears in every New Testament list of the Twelve suggests that James remained faithful to his Lord and continued to carry out his role in the apostolic band. He does not stand out like Peter or the other James or John or Andrew, but he stands faithful to his call through it all. Thus, James becomes a significant model for us, a model of faithfulness without fanfare.

Faithfulness without fanfare may be the most genuine kind of faith, according to the New Testament, for it is a faith that is not dependent on the accolades of others for its continuance. In fact, its permanence is not predicated on outward results and signs. It continues regardless of the circumstances, for it is focused on the God who remains faithful to us whatever the circumstances may be. It is easy to be faithful when rewards are forthcoming in the form of the applause of others or blessings of other sorts. The question is: will we be faithful when these other things are not there? Apparently James was. Faithful whether people were watching or not—that is the true test, faithful even when he did not get the headlines.

In the Sermon on the Mount Jesus spoke of two types of faith. According to Matthew 6:1-18, some persons practice their religion to be seen by other people. When they give alms, they sound a trumpet so that others will be sure to see. When they pray, they go to the most public place so that others will be sure to see. When they fast, they make themselves up in such a way that others will be sure to notice. Jesus clearly warned against this: "Beware of practicing your piety before others in order to be seen by them; for then you have no reward from your Father in heaven" (v. 1).

This kind of faith has all the outward appearances but none of the inner life of genuine faith. Genuine faith is not concerned that others see. Its concern is faithfulness for the sake of faithfulness, not faithfulness for the sake of fanfare. Examining the nature of our faithfulness is an ongoing operation for the disciple of Jesus, requiring that we put to ourselves some important though often painful questions. Why do I do the things that I do? If no one else knew what I was doing, would I continue to do it? Answers to questions such as these can help us determine whether we, like James the son of Alphaeus, are prepared to be faithful without fanfare.

Reconciled to Reconcile

We have already discussed the possibility that James and Matthew, both described as sons of Alphaeus, were brothers. We have also examined the possibility that James may have been an ardent Jewish nationalist. Now let us put these two observations together. If James was the brother of Matthew, and if he was an ardent Jewish nationalist, then we have in the apostolic band an example of the marvelous reconciliation that occurs when people come to know Jesus Christ as

Savior and Lord. Just think about the dramatic difference between these two men.

Matthew was a tax collector in the service of Herod Antipas, the Jewish king who was little more than a puppet of Rome. As such, Matthew was considered by Jewish nationalists to be a traitor to his own people. In the eyes of the nationalists he had sold his soul to the Romans and was little better than the scum of the earth. In fact, tax collectors were commonly lumped together with prostitutes and murderers in the minds of the people.

Then there was James, whose intense and passionate patriotism would have caused him to see Matthew in exactly the manner we have described. These two men, while possibly coming from the same family, were as different as night and day. They were as far from each other in their perspectives and outlooks as two people could possibly be. Yet, here they were together, sharing life together because they had each responded to the call of Christ in their lives.

The relationship of James and Matthew is a marvelous parable of the gospel and the impact of the gospel in the hearts and lives of people. In 2 Corinthians 5:18-19, the apostle Paul presents this gospel in a very succinct fashion. According to Paul, there are two basic elements to this gospel. First, God has reconciled us to God's self in Jesus Christ. Second, God has given to us, those who have been reconciled, the ministry of reconciliation, a reconciliation that must extend to our relationships to one another. The reconciling of relationships is not a luxury for the disciple of Jesus. Do you remember how John put it?

> Whoever says "I am in the light," while hating a brother or sister, is still in the darkness. (1 John 2:9)

> Those who say, "I love God," and hate their brothers or sisters, are liars; for those who do not love a brother or sister whom they have seen, cannot love God whom they have not seen. (1 John 4:20)

Being reconciled to others is inextricably related to being reconciled to God; the two cannot be separated.

In the Sermon on the Mount Jesus emphasized the importance of reconciliation. Do you remember what he said?

> So when you are offering your gift at the altar, if you remember that your brother or sister has something against you, leave your gift there before the altar and go; first be reconciled to your brother or sister, and then come and offer your gift. (Matt 5:23-24)

Of first importance for Jesus was the reconciling of relationships. Everything else could wait!

Apparently James had heard and responded to Jesus' teaching. Whatever may have separated him and his brother had been dealt with so that reconciliation could be a reality and they could become a model of the reconciling love of Jesus Christ. Of course, even if James and John were not brothers, this reconciliation would still have had to occur between two men who represented such diverse backgrounds, backgrounds that could not help but foster hatred and hostility between them. The disciple band is to be a community of reconciled relationships, a community in which even a James and a Matthew can come together!

A willingness to be a reconciling agent is a characteristic that should mark the life of every disciple. The Beatitudes note but one characteristic by which people will be recognized as the children of God: "Blessed are the peacemakers for they will be called children of God" (Matt 5:9). As we are about the business of peacemaking we are recognized as the children of God. This ministry of peacemaking in which we seek to initiate reconciliation in our relationships with others is the ministry that we have been given, but how eager are we to carry out this ministry? Every disciple must ask this question.

Is reconciliation needed in some of our relationships or in our churches? As James and Matthew became a model of the real power of the reconciling love of Christ, so our lives and churches should provide a living witness to this reconciling love. In an age where alienation has become the order of the day, the good news of the gospel is that reconciliation is possible, and as disciples of Jesus we are called to live in such a way that the reality of this reconciling love is made manifest for all to see!

In James, the son of Alphaeus, we meet one who was prepared to be faithful without fanfare. In this James we meet someone who had come to understand that he had been reconciled to become an agent of reconciliation. These characteristics must mark our lives if we are to be disciples of Christ, fellow travelers with James on the journey of discipleship.

Notes

[1]Latin manuscripts referring to Judas the son of James as Judas the Zealot are Vercellinis, Veronensis, Sangermanesis, and Claromontanus, which range in date from the fourth to the ninth centuries. Two manuscripts of the *Apostolic Constitutions* refer to Thaddeus as Judas the Zealot.

[2]Nicephorus, 2.40.

[3]The tradition of his preaching and subsequent martrydom in Persia is found in the *"Martyrologium Hieronymi"* (*Patrol.* 30.478).

Judas Iscariot

Biblical Texts
Matthew 10:4; 26:14-25; 27:3-10; Mark 3:19; 14:10-11;
Luke 6:16; 22:3-6; John 6:66-71; 12:1-8; 13:18-30; Acts 1:16-20

Though we learn more from the Gospels about him than we learn about any of the twelve apostles except Peter, Judas Iscariot stands out as the most enigmatic figure in the pages of the New Testament. His name has become synonymous with treachery, deceit, and betrayal. It is used in combination with other words to give the most negative connotations possible. There is the "Judas-kiss," the kiss of betrayal, and the "Judas-goat," the one who leads others astray. Parents are wont to name their children after Peter, Andrew, James, or John, but who would think of naming a child Judas?

Traitors have, of course, always received a great deal of attention. In Shakespeare's plays, for example, Shylock is as famous as Portia, Iago as Othello, Brutus as Julius Caesar, Lady MacBeth as Banquo. In our own American history there is Benedict Arnold, whose name has become synonymous with the traitor and whose life has been the subject of countless studies. After all, what makes a traitor? This question intrigues us all.

The enigma of Judas Iscariot remains very much a mystery to most of us. How, we ask ourselves, could anyone who had been so close to Jesus possibly have betrayed him? What led Judas to this tragic and fateful end? Just what do we know about him?

The name Judas Iscariot appears in all three lists of the Twelve in the synoptic Gospels (Matt 10:4; Mark 3:19; Luke 6:16), and he is mentioned as one of the Twelve in Acts 1:17. In the Synoptics, he makes no appearance until the last days of Jesus' ministry. In John's Gospel, however, he makes two earlier appearances that give us more information. According to John 12:6, Judas was the treasurer of the disciple band, an indication that he must have been respected and trusted by the other disciples. The narrative of John 13:21-30 suggests that he was given the place of honor at the Last Supper. All four Gospels recount the story of Judas' betrayal of Jesus to the Jewish authorities (Matt 26:14-16; Mark 14:10-11; Luke 22:3-6; John 13:1-2; 18:1-2), and his subsequent violent death is narrated by both Matthew (27:3-10) and Luke (Acts 1:16-20).

The name Judas represents the Greek form of the Hebrew "Judah," the name of one of Israel's sons, and a name worn with distinction by many of the heroes of Israel. Much discussion has focused on the meaning of Iscariot. Jerome, translator of the Latin Vulgate, connected Iscariot with the name Issacher, which means "gain" or "reward," and suggested that it should be understood as a reference to the covetous nature of Judas suggested by John 12:6.

Some language experts have associated Iscariot with the Greek word *hierochites*, meaning an inhabitant of Jericho, thus indicating that Judas was from that city. Syriac versions of the New Testament omit the "I" from Iscariot and read the word *scortya*, which in Latin describes a leather coat with large pockets for carrying purses and other items. Thus, the name might be suggestive of Judas' role as "keeper of the purses." Some academicians have connected Iscariot with the Greek term *sikarios*, the Greek form of the Latin *sicarius* ("dagger carrier"), used to describe a group of fanatical Jewish nationalists, thus indicating that Judas was a member of this group.

Still others have suggested that Iscariot is derived from the Aramaic word *ish*, or "man," and *kerioth*, the name of a village in Judea. It would mean something like "man of Kerioth," indicating that Judas was from that village. As far as we know, this would make Judas the only Judean among the Twelve. While none of these suggestions can be ruled out entirely, most New Testament scholars favor one of the last two interpretations.

As we have noted, Matthew, Mark, and Luke provide little information about Judas until the final fateful week of Jesus' life. In John's Gospel, however, we discover two incidents that occurred earlier in Jesus' ministry that may help us to understand Judas' actions.

The Things of God or of Humankind?
Reflection Text
John 6:66-71

John 6 begins with the story of the feeding of the 5,000 (vv. 1-13). Following the feeding, the people were coming to Jesus to "take him by force to make him king" (v. 15). No doubt many of those present perceived this miracle as a messianic sign, since according to popular tradition in the messianic age, God would once again provide manna for the people even as God had done for the people of Israel in the wilderness of Sinai. Verses 30-31 seem to confirm that this was indeed the case. Most of the crowd probably also shared the widely held view that the coming Messiah would be a Davidic king who would set up his throne in Jerusalem and drive the Roman oppressors into the sea. Thus, they were ready to take Jesus and make him king.

In response, Jesus took leave of the crowd and, after crossing the sea to Capernaum, delivered a long discourse. As he described his purpose and mission in this discourse, many of those listening began to murmur (vv. 40, 60-61). In fact, John ends this account by focusing the attention of his readers on the fact that some hearers did not believe Jesus' words: "Many of his disciples turned back and no longer went about with him" (v. 66). Jesus asked the Twelve if they were also going away. Peter responded with the confession that the disciples believed that Jesus was the Christ, the Son of the living God. To whom else, then, could they go? (vv. 68-69).

Jesus responded with an interesting question: "Did I not choose you, the twelve? Yet one of you is a devil" (v. 70). John then interpreted Jesus' question by indicating that "he was speaking of Judas son of Simon Iscariot, for he, though one of the Twelve, was going to betray him" (v. 71). Was John suggesting to us that Judas' betrayal of Jesus was somehow related to the kind of disillusionment with Jesus that caused many of his disciples to turn away from Jesus and no longer go about with him (v. 66)? These left Jesus because they were not satisfied with what Jesus had said about himself and the nature of his ministry. Was Judas' betrayal similarly a result of his unwillingness to accept the way that Jesus had chosen to accomplish that which God had sent him to do?

Another event in the Gospels has some striking parallels to the incident just described: the confrontation between Jesus and Peter at Caesarea Philippi (Matt 16:13-28). Read the story for yourself, and note any similarities that seem to appear. In the Matthean narrative Jesus asked his disciples, "Who do people say that the Son of Man is?" (v. 13). After they had shared several popular perceptions, Peter responded with the same confession found in John 6:69: "You are the Messiah, the Son of the living God" (Matt 16:16).

Immediately Jesus began to teach "his disciples that he must go to Jerusalem and undergo great suffering at the hands of the elders and chief priests and scribes, and be killed, and on the third day be raised" (v. 21). Unwilling to accept the possibility of such a scenario, Peter took Jesus aside and "began to rebuke him, saying, 'God forbid, Lord! This must never happen to you' " (v. 22). Do you remember Jesus' response to Peter? "Get behind me, Satan! You are a stumbling block to me; for you are setting your mind not on divine things but on human things" (v. 23). Note that in Matthew Jesus referred to Peter as Satan, and in John 6:70 Judas is referred to as a devil.

Was Judas' problem the same problem as that reflected in Peter's response to Jesus in Matthew? Was Judas unwilling to accept the way Jesus has chosen? Was he enamored with the things of humankind rather than the things of God? Is this what Jesus saw in Judas at the feeding of the 5,000? Would this lead to his destruction and death?

The Poor or the Purse?
Reflection Text
John 12:1-8

John 12:1-8 tells the story of the anointing of Jesus by Mary at the home of Lazarus, Mary, and Martha in Bethany. From this story we learn several interesting things. First, Judas must have been highly respected and trusted by his fellow disciples because he was entrusted with the role of keeping "the common purse" (6:6). At the same time, however, this verse suggests that things may not always be what they seem on the surface. In fact, John suggests that the trust the disciples demonstrated was a misplaced trust since Judas was pilfering the purse. Appearances can be deceiving! How much of our Christian commitment is merely appearance? How much is merely cosmetic? How deep does our commitment really run?

Second, we see Judas' extremely negative reaction to the anointing in verses 6 and 7. The oil used for the anointing was very expensive oil worth 300 denarii (a denarius was a day's wage for a common laborer). Why not sell the oil, Judas argued, and give the proceeds to the poor? Certainly this would seem to be a worthy suggestion, but John indicates that Judas' motives were not as pure as they might appear (once again, appearances can be deceiving). In fact, John suggests that Judas' concern was not so much for the poor as for the purse! The story is seen by John as another indication of the tragic tendency in Judas to focus his attention on the things of humankind rather than on the things of God!

The Fateful Choice
Reflection Texts
Matthew 26:14-16; 27:17-25; John 13:21-30

Finally, we turn to the tragic events of the last week of Judas' life. He made an agreement with the Jewish authorities to hand Jesus over to their custody (Matt 26:14-16). His reasons are impossible for us to fathom with any certainty. Through the years, many suggestions have been offered. Some persons have suggested that because he may have been the only Judean among the Twelve he had come to see himself as an outsider or outcast from the group, and, therefore, he acted in spite. Based on John 12:6, others have suggested that Judas acted mainly for the money, motivated by simple greed. If this is the case, however, it is strange that he would not have sought a greater sum of money. The amount he received was really rather small.

Some scholars have suggested that Judas was a member of the *sicarii*, that group of radical Jewish nationalists bent on the overthrow of the Romans and the establishing of an independent Jewish state. According to this scenario, Judas believed that Jesus was the Messiah who had come to usher in the Kingdom, but he was impatient with the speed with which Jesus was moving and felt that he could prompt Jesus to act by bringing the authorities against him. Others have suggested that Judas had gradually (perhaps beginning as early as the feeding of the 5,000) come to realize that Jesus' purposes were not the same as his, and his growing disillusionment with Jesus led finally to the betrayal. In the final analysis, of course, we cannot know what Judas may have been thinking.

Clearly, however, he had determined to hand Jesus over to the authorities as they were making their way to Jerusalem. By the time they gathered for the last supper, he had already struck his deal with the authorities. In the upper room, however, we find a most incredible thing occurring. As we have seen, according to John's Gospel, Jesus already knew that Judas would betray him. Still it appears that at the Last Supper, Jesus, serving as the host for the supper, invited Judas to sit in the seat of honor! Let me explain what I mean.

First, read the story in Matthew 26:17-25 and John 13:21-30. At the time of Jesus, the guests at such a dinner would recline on low couches, resting on their left elbow so as to leave the right arm free for eating. John 13:23 suggests that John was at Jesus' right, reclining on his breast. The position to the left of the host was left for the honored guest, for the host would then recline with his head resting on the breasts of the honored guest.

Three foods would be found on the Passover table: (1) a paste (made of apples, dates, pomegranates, and nuts) known as *charosheth*, which symbolized the clay from which the Israelites made bricks while they were slaves in Egypt; (2) bitter herbs (endive, horseradish, chicory, horehound, and others), which symbolized the bitterness of their slavery in Egypt; and (3) unleavened bread. At one point in the meal some of the bitter herbs were placed between two pieces of unleavened bread, dipped in the *charosheth*, and eaten. This was called the sop, and for the host to make up the sop and hand it to a guest was a signal of honor. According to John 13:26, Jesus handed the sop to Judas! Furthermore, the verbal interchange between Jesus and Judas in verse 23 was apparently a private one. Surely, if the others had heard it, they would have attempted to stop Judas rather than assuming that he was merely going to buy provisions for the feast (v. 29).

Now what is the point in all of this? Even on the night of his betrayal, Jesus reached out in love to Judas and offered him the opportunity to respond to his love and purposes. Still, Judas was more concerned with the things of humankind than with the things of God. In short, when it came down to a choice between Jesus and Judas, Judas chose Judas! He had the same opportunities, the same personal exposure to Jesus that the other eleven had, but he chose Judas. He had, at least for a time, the respect of the others; and all the while, he had the love of Jesus, even to the last. Still he chose Judas, and we wonder how he could do it. How could he choose the things of humankind rather than the things of God?

In a sense, Judas' life represents the struggle of every disciple—the struggle between commitment to the things of humankind and the things of God, and we must be careful to examine our lives at this point. Perhaps as Carlyle Marney once suggested, we have tended to make Judas a scapegoat and forgotten that it was not Judas alone who sent Jesus to Calvary.[1] Of course, the choice between the ways of humankind and the ways of God is as old as the Garden of Eden and as contemporary as today.

The temptation to which Judas succumbed confronts every disciple over and over again. It is the temptation to put self first when Jesus has called us to put the Kingdom first. Judas presents to us the clearest picture of the inevitable result of putting the things of humankind before the things of God. The temptation to which he succumbed is ever there for those who would be disciples of Jesus. May God grant that we may not be guilty of walking in his steps!

Note

[1]See "Company of Betrayers" in *The Crucible of Redemption* (Wake Forest NC: Chanticleer, 1968) 13-21.

Thomas

Biblical Texts
Matthew 10:24; Mark 3:16-19;
Luke 6:14-16; John 11:5-16; 14:1-7; 20:24-29; Acts 1:13

What is the first thing that comes to your mind when you think of the apostle Thomas? Many people would answer without hesitation: "doubting." Indeed, we have traditionally characterized this disciple of Jesus as "Doubting Thomas," but is this assessment really fair? What else do we know about this oft-maligned figure?

The name Thomas, while a familiar personal name to us, was not used as a personal name among the Jews at the time of Jesus. In both Aramaic and Hebrew it is simply an epithet meaning "the twin." By the time of the writing of the Gospels, however, it appears to have evolved into a personal name. This was probably due to the influence of the Greek name Didymas by which Thomas was also known in the churches for which John wrote (John 11:16; 20:24). Didymas, though it means "twin" in Greek, was used by the Greeks as a personal name. Possibly the attribution "the twin" was used to differentiate between this disciple and another of Jesus' disciples who bore the same name. Syriac text traditions attribute the name Judas to this disciple, calling him Judas the Twin, and in the apocryphal Gospel of Thomas he is called Didymas Judas Thomas.

Certainly if his name was Judas, one can readily understand the need for such a descriptive differentiation so that this Judas would not be confused with the other Judas in the disciple band! By the third or fourth century when the apocryphal Acts of Thomas was written, Thomas had come to be regarded as the twin of Jesus because of the mention of a Judas who was the brother of Jesus in the story of Jesus' visit to Nazareth (Mark 6:3). Such a notion, however, would seem highly unlikely.

Thomas appears in the middle of the lists of the twelve apostles found in Matthew (10:24), Mark (3:16-19), Luke (6:14-16), and Acts (1:13). However, Matthew, Mark, Luke, and Acts tell us nothing else about him. We must turn to the Gospel of John for insights into his character. In this Gospel he appears in three significant passages, passages that enable us to form a true picture of Thomas.

Faithful unto Death
Reflection Text
John 11:8-16

Our first glimpse into the character of Thomas is found in John 11. According to John 10:22-42, Jesus had been teaching in the Temple in Jerusalem during the Feast of Dedication, a Jewish festival commemorating the rededication of the temple in 164 B.C.E. after its desecration by Antiochus Epiphanes. In response to his teaching about his relationship with God, "the Jews took up stones again to stone him" (v. 31), believing that he was teaching blasphemy. When Jesus attempted to clarify further his teaching "they tried to arrest him again, but he escaped from their hands" (v. 39). This incident was, of course, not the first such confrontation with the religious leadership.

John 8:59 describes a similar incident when Jesus was teaching in the temple at the Feast of Tabernacles. In terms of his relationship with the religious leadership, Jesus' ministry had reached a crisis point. The time for the final confrontation had not yet come, so Jesus "went away again across the Jordan to the place where John had been baptizing earlier, and he remained there" (10:40-42). His "hour" had not yet come, and across the Jordan the Jewish authorities had no jurisdiction.

Shortly after this incident, Jesus learned of the illness of his dear friend Lazarus. Lazarus and his sisters, Mary and Martha, lived in Bethany, a village about two miles from Jerusalem over the Mount of Olives. Jesus did not go to Bethany immediately upon hearing of Lazarus' illness, but announced to his disciples his intention to go. He planned to re-cross the Jordan and "go to Judea again" (11:7).

His disciples must have been shocked! Bethany was the village through which most pilgrims passed as they made their way up to Jerusalem and the temple. The authorities would most certainly be on the lookout for Jesus there. An attempt to visit Lazarus there must have seemed suicidal! No wonder the disciples seemed determined to persuade Jesus to remain where he (and they) would be safe. At this point, in the midst of the reluctance of his fellow disciples to go with Jesus, Thomas stepped forward to say, "Let us also go, that we may die with him" (11:16).

Thomas' statement suggests several things. It reveals the extent of danger that the disciples must have felt. He clearly perceived the dangers that loomed before Jesus and anyone who would go with him, very possibly death. Nevertheless, Thomas was a person of intense loyalty and courage. He expected the worst, yet he was still prepared to follow his master. He was not about to abandon Jesus in this difficult hour in order that he might remain in a safe haven across the Jordan. Was this the response of a doubter? Why was Thomas willing to die with Jesus if necessary? Was it not because of his love for and commitment to him? Was it not because Thomas had realized that for a disciple there is no real existence apart from his master?

This picture of Thomas is quite different from the Thomas we normally remember. Here is Thomas who stands before us as a model of bravery and courage, but more than this, as a model of genuine discipleship. The true disciple is prepared to go all the way with the master, even to death. The true disciple realizes that no life exists apart from the master who gives life. When a disciple recognizes this, there is no limit to what he/she can accomplish for the Master. Thomas was prepared to be faithful to his master, faithful unto death! This is the mark of genuine discipleship.

Concerned to Know the Truth
Reflection Text
John 14:1-7

Thomas played a significant role when Jesus and the disciples gathered in the upper room in Jerusalem where Jesus planned to prepare the disciples for his impending departure and death. He sought to comfort them by revealing to them that he was going to prepare a place for them in the Father's house, that he would come again for them, and that where he was going they would go also. "And you know," he said, "the way to the place where I am going" (John 14:4). At this point Thomas interrupted Jesus. "Lord, we do not know where you are going. How can we know the way?" To this question Jesus responded, "I am the way, and the truth, and the life" (v. 6).

Thanks be to God for Thomas' question that provided the occasion for Jesus' magnificent and telling response! Thomas stands before us here as one who is a seeker for truth. He stands before us as one who is a disciple in the truest sense of the word, for the word disciple literally means "learner." Thomas simply could not live with an unanswered question. He was not satisfied just to listen to Jesus and pass over those things that he did not understand. Unable to grasp the meaning of Jesus' words, he openly confessed his ignorance and put his question to Jesus. He pursued the issue until he understood. Not interested in just listening, he wanted to learn. And, oh what he learned!

Jesus' response to Thomas' question might be paraphrased in this way: "Whatever happens, Thomas, you have me! And I am the way, the truth, and the life." In the final analysis, a set of directions does not make the way clear, nor does a philosophical treatise make clear the truth. The way, the truth, the life is found in the person of Jesus. In a personal relationship with this Jesus we are able to know the way to go, the truth to believe, and the life we were created to live. Jesus' words to Thomas make it crystal clear. Thomas was a seeker for truth, a disciple in the truest sense of the word.

Reluctant Realist
Reflection Text
John 20:24-29

We come at last to that incident in Thomas' life with which we are most familiar. Jesus had been crucified. After the resurrection he had appeared to his disciples who were gathered in the upper room on the evening of the first day of the week (John 20:19). Thomas, however, was not present. No doubt distraught and disillusioned, he had stolen away somewhere to be alone with his grief. When the other disciples told him that they had seen the risen Lord, he refused to believe them without incontrovertible evidence. "Unless I see the mark of the nails in his hands and put my finger in the mark of the nails and my hand in his side, I will not believe" (v. 25). These words, of course, provide the basis for our perception of Thomas as "doubting Thomas," but we should consider two things at this point.

First, try to imagine yourself in Thomas' shoes. Standing on this side of Easter, we can easily stand in judgment of Thomas, but we must remember that Thomas did not have the benefit of 2,000 years of testimony to the reality of the resurrection. All he knew was that Jesus had been brutally killed. Why should he believe this news about a resurrection? If there was to be a resurrection, it would be on the last day, and this was certainly not the last day. Who among us would have believed it? Perhaps it would help to think of it this way. What do we think of people in our day who talk about people being raised from the dead? Is Thomas' reluctance to believe really all that surprising?

Second, remember that Thomas was not the only doubter. Actually, none of the disciples believed the announcement of the women when they came to tell the disciples that Jesus had been raised from the dead (Mark 16:11, 14). Luke 24:41 speaks of their continuing disbelief even when he appeared to them! If we speak of "doubting" Thomas, then perhaps we must also speak of "doubting" Peter, "doubting" James, and "doubting" John.

Thomas' doubt is not surprising, and Jesus did not condemn him for it. He knew that once Thomas had fought his way through the wilderness of his doubt, he would be an even more committed disciple, and of course, he was. Frederick Buechner put it well: "Doubts are the ants in the pants of faith."[1] Doubt forces us to struggle with significant issues and can spur us on to deeper faith.

Eight days after Jesus' first appearance to the disciples in the upper room, the disciples were gathered there again. This time Thomas was present. Jesus appeared in their midst and invited Thomas to place his finger in the mark of the nails and to place his hand in his side. Thomas' response has been called the loftiest, grandest confession of faith in the pages of the New Testament. "My Lord and my God" (John 20:28). It was not just "Lord and God." It was "*my* Lord and *my* God!"

Using the personal pronoun, Thomas made it clear that it was his conviction and faith that Jesus was, in fact, God incarnate! Jesus calls every person to make this confession. "Have you believed because you have seen me? Blessed are those who have not seen and yet have come to believe" (v. 29). Upon this confession the faith and life of the church rests. Upon the foundation of this confession the life of the disciple must be built.

Notice two things about Thomas' experience. First, his confession was the result of a personal encounter with Jesus, a first-hand experience of the power and presence of the living Christ. In the final analysis, all people need is a personal encounter with the living Christ, for he is the way, the truth, and the life. To know about Jesus is not enough; one must know the person Jesus.

Second, note that Thomas made his discovery of the living Christ in the company of other believers. Here is an important reminder of the significance of the church, the community of faith, in the life of the believer. Listen to these powerful words from the pen of Landrum Leavell:

> It is more likely that you'll recognize who Jesus is if you're among Christians than when you are with pagans or even by yourself. I have a real suspicion of those who say that they can get closer to God out fishing or on the golf course than they can with the company of believers. Jesus didn't set up his kingdom for all of us to be little "lone ranger" Christians, everyone off by himself, worshipping God the way he sees fit. Jesus Christ set it up for his followers to be part

of the company of believers and unitedly to spread the gospel to the end of the earth.[2]

This is not to say that one cannot find Christ in solitude and silence. Still, it is more likely in the company of believers. For Thomas, assurance came, not while he was away by himself, but when he was gathered with other believers. Yes, Thomas had his doubts, but together with fellow believers he came to know the reality of the resurrection. When he discovered this reality, he responded with the same courage and loyalty that he had demonstrated when he announced his resolve to go back to Judea with Jesus even if it meant that he would die with him there.

According to Eusebius, after the ascension of Jesus, Thomas was assigned the region of Parthia as his mission field.[3] The apocryphal *Acts of Thomas,* which dates from the third or fourth century C.E., says that Thomas took the gospel to India and was martyred there. To this day, the Christians of Saint Thomas in India trace their origins to the mission of Thomas.

A careful examination of the New Testament evidence about Thomas takes us far beyond our traditional perspective on this faithful follower of Jesus. We are forced to admit that the marvel is not that Thomas could ever have doubted. He did not have the benefit of 2,000 Easters and four written Gospels. The marvel is that Thomas was prepared to die with Jesus even before he knew the good news of Easter. May God grant to us the courage and commitment to be so faithful to Jesus that we are prepared to die for him, so desirous of understanding his word that we are ready to learn from him, and so eager to boldly confess our faith that we will join with Thomas in announcing to the world that Jesus is *our* Lord and *our* God!

Notes

[1]Frederick Buechner, *Wishful Thinking* (New York: Harper & Row, 1973) 20.

[2]Landrum Leavell, *Twelve Who Followed Jesus* (Nashville TN: Broadman, 1975) 56.

[3]Eusebius, *Ecclesiastical History*, 3.1.

Faithful to the End

Biblical Texts
Matthew 27:32-56; 28:1-10;
Mark 15:21-41; 16:1-8; Luke 8:1-3; 23:49, 55; 24:1-11

U ntil very recent times the suggestion that women were among the first disciples of Jesus has received very little attention outside the New Testament. Notice that I said outside the New Testament, for the New Testament itself bears clear testimony to the fact that women were among Jesus' first disciples, and that these women had a significant impact on the life of the early church. Indeed, their lives are set before us in the gospels as models of faithful discipleship, especially in the Gospel of John. While little explicit attention is given to individual women in the synoptic Gospels, the presence of women disciples can nevertheless be clearly seen.

Faithful in Galilee
Reflection Texts
Selected texts from Mark; Luke 8:1-3

In the Gospel of Luke we discover the first direct evidence that women followed Jesus as disciples during the days of his Galilean ministry. Before we examine this evidence further, however, it may be helpful to remember that there were disciples other than the Twelve. A quick examination of several passages from Luke's gospel makes this clear. For example, Luke 6:13 tells us that Jesus "called his disciples and chose twelve of them." Again in Luke 6:17 we read about "a great crowd of his disciples." Then, of course, there is Luke's account of the sending out of the seventy disciples in Luke 10:1ff. Even if the Twelve are included in this number, we must allow for at least fifty-eight more!

Now let us turn to the evidence that some of these disciples were women. According to Luke 8:1-3, as Jesus journeyed from town to town and village to village in Galilee proclaiming the Good News, he was accompanied by the Twelve and a number of women. Three of the women are mentioned by name: Mary Magdalene, from whom Jesus had cast out seven demons; Joanna, whose husband Chuza apparently acted as a manager of the estate of Herod Antipas, the tetrach of

Galilee; and Susanna. Luke states clearly, however, that these three were not the only women. "Many others" remain unnamed. (Note at this point that it is not uncommon for three of the male disciples—Peter, James, and John—to be mentioned quite often to the exclusion of the other nine. One cannot help but wonder whether the mention of the three women in this text is analogous.) Luke notes that these women "provided for" the disciple band out of their own resources.

The description of the women providing for the disciples from their own resources has significant theological overtones and sets them before us as persons who were demonstrating significant characteristics of discipleship. In fact, by the time Luke was writing this account, the word he used to refer to the service of these women (the Greek verb *diakonein*) had come to be a kind of technical term for discipleship. The importance of serving the disciple band from one's own resources is clearly seen in Acts, which forms the second part of Luke's account of early Christianity. In fact, this kind of "service" characterizes the *koinonia* of the early church in Jerusalem. The descriptions of this community of disciples in Acts 2:44-45 and 4:32–5:11 make this crystal clear. In this community "All who believed were together and had all things in common . . . so that no one was in need" (2:44). In the second of these passages Barnabas is set before us as an example of one who, like the women of Luke 8:3, served the community of faith from his own means.

While Mark and Matthew make no explicit mention of the women disciples until their accounts of Jesus' death, some implicit evidence appears earlier in their narrative. In Mark 4:10-11, for example, we find Jesus privately teaching those "around him" together with the Twelve. In Mark such private teaching is confined to Jesus' disciples. Interestingly, just a few verses earlier in 3:31-35, Jesus had defined his family as those who were "around him," those who were sitting at his feet, listening to his teaching and doing God's will. These, he said, were his "brother and sister and mother." Jesus made it clear that not only "brothers," but also "sisters" made up those "around him."

Notice also how often Mark uses women as models of faith. Think, for example, of the woman with the issue of blood (5:25-34), the Syro-Phoenecian woman (7:24-30), and the woman who anointed Jesus in preparation for his death (14:3-9). While again and again the faith of such women is affirmed and applauded by Jesus, the faith of the Twelve is characterized by the continual misunderstanding of the nature of Jesus' message and ministry (for example, 8:31-33; 9:33-37; 10:35-45). Finally, at the cross Mark speaks of the

> women looking on from a distance . . . these used to follow him and provided for him when he was in Galilee; these were women who had come up with him to Jerusalem. (15:40-41)

Faithful at the Cross
Reflection Texts
Matthew 27:32-56; Mark 15:21-41; Luke 23:49, 55

Each of the Gospel writers makes it clear that the women who had followed Jesus *in* Galilee, also followed him *from* Galilee to Jerusalem and all the way to the cross. We have already noted how Mark records the presence of these women at Calvary. He mentions by name Mary Magdalene, Mary the mother of James the Younger and Joses, and Salome. Matthew affirms the testimony of Mark and mentions the same three women by name (Salome and the mother of the sons of Zebedee were likely the same person). In both Mark and Matthew the women are characterized by two Greek verbs that had come to be technical terms for Jesus' disciples: they "followed" (*akolouthein*) and "served" (*diakonein*) Jesus. Luke agrees that "the women who had followed him from Galilee" (23:49) were there.

These texts force a haunting question upon the reader. Where were the Twelve when Jesus died on the cross at Calvary? While Luke suggests that "all his acquaintances" (23:49) were there, of those who had followed him from Galilee, only the women are mentioned. The fact is that none of the Gospels (with the possible exception of John who places the beloved disciple there) give any indication that any of the Twelve were there when their Lord was crucified!

Furthermore, we are forced to ask where the Twelve were after Jesus' death? In a culture in which the primary duty of disciples was to care for the body of their teacher in death, where were the Twelve? According to Luke, only the women were there when Jesus' body was removed from the cross. They followed as his body was taken to the tomb, they "saw the tomb and how his body was laid" (23:55). Matthew captures the scene with powerful pathos when he tells us that after Joseph of Arimathea had sealed the door of the tomb, "Mary Magdalene and the other Mary were there, sitting opposite the tomb" (27:61). Truly it can be said that these women were faithful to the end! One cannot help but ask with the poet Thomas Carlisle:

Who were the real disciples?
Those who served,
who cared how Jesus felt,
who understood the other side of failure,
who followed to the cross,
who shared the pain,
who traveled to the tomb,
with tears and spices,
and met the miracle of Easter morning.
They were the real disciples.[1]

Faithful in the Garden . . . and Beyond
Reflection Texts
Matthew 28:1-10; Mark 16:1-8; Luke 24: 1-11

The "miracle of Easter morning" brings the New Testament's most significant affirmation of women. The startling fact is that in all four of the Gospels the incredible "good news" of the resurrection is first announced to the women! Mark describes how Mary Magdalene and Mary the mother of James and Salome were the first to discover the empty tomb, how they were addressed by a young man dressed in white who announced to them the glorious good news: "He has been raised, he is not here" (16:6), and how they were commissioned by this heavenly messenger to go and tell the others. Matthew adds that as they started from the tomb "with fear and great joy" (28:8), running to tell the other disciples, suddenly Jesus himself stood in their path and commissioned them to go and tell the brethren.

Luke's account is particularly interesting at this point. Confronted at the tomb by two messengers in "dazzling apparel," they were frightened and bowed their faces to the ground. Do you remember the words that the messengers then spoke?

Why do you look for the living among the dead? . . . Remember how
he told you, while he was still in Galilee, that the Son of man must
be handed over to sinners, and be crucified, and on the third day rise
again. (24:5-6)

Then Luke tells us that *"they* remembered" (24:8)! Not only had these women been with Jesus in Galilee, they had been there on those occasions when Jesus had spoken of what lay before him in Jerusalem. Now take a moment and look at Luke 9:44-45, 17:22-25, and 18:31-34. These passages refer to private times, times when Jesus withdrew with his disciples to teach them of these things and their significance. According to Luke, the women were there!

The witness of the Gospels is clear. Women were the first to discover the empty tomb. According to Mark and Luke, the announcement of the resurrection was first made to the women. Matthew and John indicate that the resurrected Jesus first appeared to the women. According to all of the Gospel accounts, the women were the first to be commissioned to announce this good news. In fact, they would be the very ones to announce the news to the other disciples. Once again, the Gospels make it clear that the women were faithful to the task. They had been faithful to Jesus to what seemed like the dreadful end, but that "end" was only the beginning, and their faithfulness was rewarded as they became witnesses to "the miracle of Easter morning."

Throughout the Gospels the women stand before us as models of genuine discipleship. They were loyal and faithful in times of joy and trial, through miracle and mourning. They were continually acting as witnesses to the person and work of Jesus, accepting the nature of his ministry even though it included suffering and death. They served their Lord and his followers faithfully, faithful to the end. Once again, Thomas Carlisle has captured the power and the pathos of these women disciples of Jesus.

> The women disciples
> are not dramatic
> and exciting
> like the men.
> None betrayed him,
> none denied him,
> none insisted on misunderstanding
> in the accounts we treasure.
> They did not hesitate
> to argue or to offer
> their own opinions
> but they were always ready
> to recognize the tenor
> of his teachings
> and take him seriously
> at full face value
> and follow with tenacity
> and devotion
> no matter the cost.[2]

Notes

[1]Thomas John Carlisle, *Beginning with Mary: Women of the Gospels in Portrait* (Grand Rapids MI: Eerdmans, 1986) 59.
   [2]Ibid.

Mary and Martha

Biblical Texts
Luke 10:38-42; John 11:1-44; 12:1-8

The village of Bethany was a significant place. Located just over the Mount of Olives, not more than two miles from Jerusalem, it was a prominent stopping-off point for pilgrims coming up from Jericho on their way to the holy city. Bethany was certainly a significant place for Jesus, not only because of where it was, but also because of who was there. In Bethany he found open hearts and an open home. He found a warm welcome on numerous occasions in the home of Mary, Martha, and their brother Lazarus.

Of these three persons, our attention has generally tended to focus on Lazarus, despite the fact that we know the least about him. In fact, he is completely passive in the narratives in which he appears. The Gospels tell us much more about his sisters, Mary and Martha, from whom we can learn much about discipleship. In fact, Mary and Martha are featured in three major stories in the Gospel narratives, each of which contributes a significant truth about the journey of discipleship.

The One Necessary Thing
Reflection Text
Luke 10:38-42

We first meet Mary and Martha on the occasion of a dinner that Jesus had been invited to attend in their home in Bethany. Martha was busy with the preparations for the meal. Mary, on the other hand, had taken a seat "at the Lord's feet and listened to what he was saying" (Luke 10:39). Her posture, sitting at the feet of Jesus, and the fact that she was listening to his words both suggest that this was a teaching setting. In other words, Jesus was giving religious instruction as they waited for the meal to begin.

In first-century Palestine, such a setting was no place for a woman. Religious instruction was simply not open to women. Women were meant for labor, not for learning. Thus, to say that Mary's behavior was unconventional is something of an understatement. Her behavior was incredible! There she was, a woman, trespassing on the sacred teacher-disciple relationship. She was assuming a role that belonged to men only. She was clearly violating the role of women in her day and time.

Of course, we must remember that Mary was not alone in this violation. The fact is that Jesus was perfectly willing for Mary to be there. He made no effort to turn her away, and by his behavior he affirmed her right, indeed the right of every woman, to gather around him as his disciple. She had as much right to be there learning from Jesus, hearing his words, as any of the others.

Martha's reaction to this situation is not surprising. Aside from the unconventional and perhaps somewhat embarrassing nature of her sister's behavior, there was the business of the preparation of the meal that had to be completed. So Martha sought Jesus' help in an effort to draft Mary from the study back to the kitchen. Jesus' response is most telling. "Martha, Martha, you are worried and distracted by many things; there is need of only one thing" (vv. 40-41a). Some biblical teachers have suggested that Jesus may have been saying that one dish was enough for the meal and that Martha need not trouble herself with further elaborate preparations. In this case, the one necessary thing would refer to the one dish for the meal. The rest of Jesus' statement, however, suggests that he had something else in mind. "Mary," he continued, "has chosen the better part, which will not be taken away from her" (v. 41b).

Jesus' words suggest that "the better part" refers to his teaching to which Mary had chosen to give her attention. If this is the case, then the one thing that was necessary was to hear the words of Jesus. The food that Martha was preparing was important, but it could only impact those present in a temporary way. The words of Jesus, however, would have eternal significance for all who would hear them.

Mary had taken her place at the feet of Jesus. She assumed the posture of a disciple. She had realized that, in the final analysis, nothing is more important than giving attention to the words of Jesus. This is not to say, however, that there are no other important things or that what Martha was doing was unimportant. It is to recognize that all other things can only be seen in their proper perspective and can take their proper place when seen in light of the word of the Lord. Apart from a hearing and an understanding of that word, priorities will be skewed and ultimately the one necessary thing neglected. The words of Jesus give to everything its proper place in our lives.

Mary sat at the feet of Jesus in this story. In so doing she stands before us as a model of the disciple's commitment to hear and understand the words of Jesus. There is an interesting parallel in Mark's account of the call of the Twelve. Read Mark 3:13-14. Do you notice anything interesting about Mark's description of what they were called to do? Jesus called them "to be with him, to be sent out to proclaim the message, and to have authority to cast out demons." The sequence is striking to me.

The first order of business for the disciples was "to be with him," for only when they had been with him, only after they had listened to his words and spent time in his presence, would they be able to carry out the rest of their mission. In fact, it is not until Mark 6 that Jesus sends them out! The implications are clear. Until we have taken the time to sit at Christ's feet, all of our activity is likely to be "much ado about nothing." Only one thing is necessary, and when that one thing is cared for, all other things will take their proper place.

The Great Confession
Reflection Text
John 11:1-44

We meet Mary and Martha again in John 11. Their brother Lazarus was ill. They had sent a messenger to inform Jesus of the situation. Jesus had chosen not to return to Bethany immediately, but indicated that "this illness does not lead to death" (v. 4). The next few days would present the ultimate challenge to the faithfulness of Mary and Martha for, in spite of what Jesus had said, Lazarus died. Imagine how they must have felt. Imagine what they must have thought. Was Jesus wrong? It must have seemed that way to them. What else could they think? If Jesus had been wrong about this, how could they be sure he was right about other things? How could they trust his teaching?

We could hardly blame Mary and Martha if they had reacted in this way, but when Jesus arrived in Bethany a few days later, he found faith and trust alive in Mary and Martha. Hearing that Jesus was coming, Martha rushed from town to greet him. The dialogue that followed reveals an unusual depth of commitment. Clearly Martha had already identified Jesus with the source of life. She had discovered in him one who had the power to give life. "Lord, if you had been here, my brother would not have died" (v. 21). Furthermore, she had recognized that in Jesus, God was at work. "Even now I know that God will give you whatever you ask from him" (v. 22). Somehow Martha had realized that God's purposes were being accomplished in the life and ministry of this Nazarene.

In response to these expressions of faith, Jesus made the most astounding claim:

> I am the resurrection and the life. Those who believe in me, even though they die, will live, and everyone who lives and believes in me will never die. (vv. 25-26)

Martha already believed in a coming resurrection, a resurrection that would occur at the last day. She knew that then her brother would be raised from death. Now Jesus was asking her to believe that he was the source of life, that in him the resurrection had come into the present! He put the question point-blank in verse 26: "Do you believe this?"

The claim was incredible—too incredible to believe. Nevertheless, Martha believed and responded with the most dramatic confession up to this point in the Gospel of John: "Lord, I believe that you are the Messiah, the Son of God, the one coming into the world" (v. 27). The significance of this passage becomes even clearer when we turn to Mark 8:27-30 where Peter's confession of faith at Caesarea Philippi is recorded. Do you see the similarities?

In Mark's Gospel this is the primary confession of faith and the pivotal point in the narrative. This confession must be made by everyone who would be a disciple of Jesus. In the Synoptics (Matthew, Mark, and Luke) it is made by Peter. In John (whose narrative does not contain Peter's confession at Caesarea Philippi) it is made by Martha. As Peter's confession stands as the pivotal midpoint in Mark, so Martha's confession stands at the climactic midpoint in John. Thus, in John's Gospel, the proclamation of Jesus' identity is made by Martha. Hers is an incredible confession that affirms an incredible claim. Nevertheless, along with Martha, we must believe it.

Doing as Jesus Did
Reflection Text
John 12:1-8

In this final incident the focus falls on Mary. It occurred six days before the Passover. Once again Jesus had come to dine with his faithful friends in Bethany. During the meal Mary anointed the feet of Jesus with a pint of an expensive perfume called nard. She completed the act by wiping his feet with her hair, a beautiful expression of love and devotion. She offered her most precious, perhaps her most costly, possession in tribute to her Lord.

This story sets before us the two ways of life that are open to all. Did you notice Judas' response to Mary's deed? According to John, while masquerading in the clothing of concern for others, it was based solely on selfish interest and desire! Ultimately, you see, there are only two ways: (1) the way of Jesus in which one dies to self and lives to God and (2) the way of the world in which one dies to God and lives to self. One way leads to life; the other way leads to death. One way is modeled by Mary; the other way is modeled by Judas.

In the course of John's Gospel, Mary's actions take on a twofold significance. While modeling the way of sacrificial service that is fundamental to the life of a disciple, she had at the same time announced her understanding of the hour that Jesus approached. The cross was looming on the horizon. Calvary stood before them. For this purpose Jesus had come, and Mary was willing to affirm the way of the cross. She had anointed him for his death.

Remember at this point that, according to the Synoptics, the Twelve demonstrated again and again on the journey to Jerusalem that they were unwilling to accept the possibility of Jesus' suffering and death. In Mark 8, when Jesus begins to teach the disciples that he must suffer and die, Peter will not hear of it. In Mark 9, when Jesus speaks of his death for a second time, the apostles are discussing their relative positions in the soon-to-be-established kingdom—no thoughts of suffering and death. When Jesus returns to this topic for a third time in Mark 10, James and John demonstrate that they still have not accepted Jesus' fate as they jockey for positions of prestige and power. All along the way, while they are ready to don the crown, they are unwilling to conceive of the cross.

While imprisoned in the Tower of London, William Penn composed a classic on Christian discipleship: *No Cross, No Crown.* Perhaps Mary had come to understand. There is no way to Easter without passing through Good Friday. This was not true just for Jesus, but is the case for anyone who would be his disciple.

If any want to become my followers, let them deny themselves and take up their cross and follow me. For those who want to save their life will lose it, and those who lose their life for my sake, and for the sake of the gospel, will save it. (Mark 8:34-35)

Mary and Martha:

— sisters who were as significant as any of the brethren in the life of Jesus
— sisters who teach us of the need for commitment to hearing the word of Jesus
— sisters who teach us the need for believing the incredible claims of Jesus and boldly confessing our faith in him
— sisters who teach us of the need to commit ourselves to the way of Jesus, which was for him and is for us the way of the cross.

The First Evangelist

Biblical Text
John 4:1-42

The Gospel of John is unique in many ways. It records a great deal of information about Jesus that is not found in any of the other Gospels. It also tells us much about the disciples of Jesus that none of the other Gospel writers record. In the opening verses of his gospel, John sets before us the nature of discipleship. After the prologue (1:1-18), the narrative begins in 1:19-51 with the story of John the Baptist and the call of two pairs of disciples: (1) Andrew and Peter and (2) Philip and Nathanael. From their stories we learn that disciples are persons who follow Jesus (vv. 35-39), believe his word (vv. 9-13), and bear witness to who he is (vv. 40-51). Notice, however, that John gives very little attention to the twelve apostles in his narrative. In fact, the concept of apostle seems to have little importance for him. For the writer of this Gospel, discipleship—not apostleship—is the important category.

Interestingly enough, this writer, who gives little attention to the Twelve, gives a great deal of attention to the role of women in the ministry of Jesus. In fact, John sets a number of women before his readers as model disciples. The most significant of these are the Samaritan woman in chapter 4, Mary and Martha in chapters 11 and 12, and Mary Magdalene in chapters 19 and 20. Let us turn our attention now to the story of the Samaritan woman.

Receiving the Revelation
Reflection Text
John 4:1-26

The story of Jesus' encounter with the Samaritan woman is an astonishing one in many respects. That Jesus would choose to travel the ridge road through Samaria is in itself surprising. As John 4:10 suggests, most Jews (especially those concerned with traditional piety) would have chosen a route that would bypass Samaria completely, since religious Jews held Samaritans in contempt, considering them to be religious apostates (see 2 Kgs 17:24-34). Nevertheless, Jesus, unpredictable as ever, chose the Samaritan way.

As they passed through Samaria, Jesus and the disciples stopped at Jacob's Well at Sychar. Weary from travel, Jesus sat down beside the well to rest while the disciples went into the city to buy food. A Samaritan woman came to the well to draw water. Her appearance there at midday (John 4:6) may suggest that she was, or at least felt that she was, ostracized from the other women of the city who would most likely visit the well in the early morning or late evening. When Jesus asked her for a drink, she was astonished that this male Jew would ask her, a woman and a Samaritan woman at that, for a drink from her cup. His behavior ran counter to all that she had come to understand about the Jews.

Of course, she was not the only one who was surprised by Jesus' behavior. When Jesus' disciples returned from the market, they "were astonished that he was speaking with a woman" (4:27). Notice that the text does not say "the" woman but "a" woman. The very idea that Jesus would be talking to any woman in public was beyond their comprehension. Men simply did not speak to women in public, not even to their wives. Certainly no rabbi would speak to a woman in public! Yet, this rabbi to whom the disciples had committed themselves was speaking to a woman in public; and this was not just any woman, this was a Samaritan woman! Once again Jesus will not be bound by our stereotypes and will have nothing to do with those attitudes that might restrict our openness to others or their response to him.

Gradually, as Jesus and the woman talked, he began to reveal his identity. He was greater than Jacob who gave her ancestors the well, for he offered a spring of water that wells up to eternal life (4:10-15). He was, in fact, a prophet because he knew all about her (vv. 16-19). He spoke to her of a time when people will know all things and worship in spirit and in truth. She knew that such a day would come with the arrival of the Messiah. Christ responded with a clear statement of his identity: "I am he, the one who is speaking to you" (vv. 20-26). Thus, Jesus revealed his identity to a woman, and that woman was a woman of Samaria!

Responding to the Revelation
Reflection Text
John 4:28-29, 39

Having heard Jesus' witness about himself, the woman responded immediately. She "left her water jar and went back to the city" (John 4:28) from which she had come to tell the people about Jesus. There is a striking similarity here between her response to Jesus and that of the other disciples. According to Mark 1:16-20, when Simon and Andrew heard Jesus' call, "immediately they left their nets and followed him." Similarly, when Jesus found Levi sitting in the tax office and called to him, he left the tax office and followed. So when the Samaritan woman was confronted by Jesus, she "left her water jar," which represented her business.

The pattern is clearly the same. Hearing the call to discipleship, we must be willing to leave whatever we are doing. We must recognize that one priority takes precedence over all others. In the Sermon on the Mount Jesus set it clearly before us. We must seek first the kingdom of God and God's righteousness (Matt 6:33). All other allegiances must give way to this allegiance. All other commitments must give way to this commitment. This is the meaning of discipleship.

The Samaritan woman "left her water jar," went back to town, and began to tell others about Jesus. Once again the pattern is a familiar one. In his narrative of the call of the first disciples in John 1:35-51, John described how, after discovering the identity of Jesus, Andrew went immediately to tell his brother Simon, and Philip went immediately to share the news with his friend Nathanael. The same is true for a disciple of Jesus. To be a disciple of Jesus is to bear witness to who Jesus is, just as the Samaritan woman did.

The results of her witness are striking. Those who heard her witness "went out of the city and were coming to him." In fact, John makes it clear in verse 39 that "many Samaritans from that city believed in him because of the woman's testimony." This is a most significant statement, for it has a striking parallel in John 17:20. This seventeenth chapter of John is sometimes referred to as "the High Priestly Prayer of Jesus." It was his prayer for the disciples he uttered in the upper room on the night before his arrest.

In this "High Priestly" prayer, Jesus prayed not only for the disciples gathered around him, but also for those persons of every age who will be his disciples. Listen carefully to his words: "I ask not only on the behalf of these (that is, for those gathered with him there), but also on behalf of those who will believe in me through their word." How had the Samaritans come to believe in Jesus? They had come to believe in Jesus "through her word." John seemed to understand the Samaritan woman to be a model of what every disciple of Jesus must be: a witness to who he is so that others may also come to know and believe.

This truth is made even clearer when we examine John 4:31-38. Notice how this little interlude that recounts a dialogue between Jesus and the disciples is placed between two verses that speak of the effect of the witness of the Samaritan woman. In verse 30 we are told of the many persons who came to Jesus, and in verse 39 of the many who believed in him. Between these two statements in verses 30-39, Jesus made it clear that the nourishment that sustains is found in doing the will of God and accomplishing "his word." He described this work in terms of bringing in the harvest from the fields that "are ripe for harvest" (v. 35). In fact, Jesus said that he had sent the disciples to do this, just as the Samaritan woman had done! In so doing she has become a model for all other disciples. She is the example of what disciples are called to do, and when they do this, many persons will come to Christ and believe in him through their word too.

What an astonishing story! Unfortunately, for many years we have only attended to the nature of the life of the Samaritan before her encounter with Jesus. What happened when she met Jesus and because she met Jesus is most important. In this story, Jesus revealed himself as the Messiah to a woman of Samaria. Indeed, he revealed that he is the "I am." As such, he is indeed "the Savior of the world." The woman had received his revelation and believed in him. In fact, she left everything to bear witness to him before others. Jesus accepted her witness and rejoiced in its results. He recognized her response as a realization of his own mission and saw it as a model for the mission of every disciple. Indeed, Christ has set a woman before us as the first evangelist!

Mary Magdalene

Biblical Texts
Luke 8:2; John 19:25; 20:1-18

Of all the women mentioned in the New Testament as followers of Jesus, none seems to have had more significance for the early church than Mary Magdalene. Her name appears first in every listing of these women in the synoptic Gospels (Mark 15:40, 47; 16:1; Matt 27:56, 61; Luke 8:2; 24:10), and the memory of her ministry seems to have been carefully preserved. As in the case of the Samaritan woman, however, our picture of this significant woman tends to be determined by our perceptions of her life before she met Jesus rather than her life after this life-transforming encounter. In fact, our perceptions of this Mary's life before she met Jesus have for the most part been based on what is probably an erroneous identification of her with the well-known "sinner" who anointed Jesus in the house of Simon the Pharisee.

Since this story is found immediately prior to the mention of Mary Magdalene in Luke 8:1-3, many Christians have assumed that this woman was, in fact, Mary Magdalene. Thus, Mary has generally been described as a woman of "ill repute." We have no evidence, however, to support this identification. Luke gives no name to the woman in Simon's house, and we have no reason to think that he understood it to have been Mary. It is hard to understand why he felt it necessary to identify Mary as the one "from whom seven demons had gone out" when he simply could have pointed to the preceding story. In fact, if the placement of the story is the strongest argument for identifying the woman as Mary, one might suggest that she could just as well have been Joanna or Susanna, who are also mentioned in Luke 8:2.

When Luke first mentions Mary Magdalene in 8:2, he identifies her as the one "from whom seven demons had gone out." This statement is obviously included to identify Mary, which would be unnecessary if he had already introduced her in the passage immediately preceding this. It seems, therefore, that Mary Magdalene was known in the early church, not as the "sinner" who had anointed Jesus' feet, but as the woman "from whom seven demons had gone out." In fact, this is all we know of her prior to her meeting with Jesus. Let us then concentrate on her life after this meeting and the significant role she played according to the Gospel narratives as one of the first disciples. We will look first at the portrayal of Mary in the Synoptics, then at the more detailed presentation in the Gospel of John.

Reconciled to Reconcile
Reflection Texts
Luke 8:2; 2 Corinthians 5:17-20

We have already seen that Luke describes Mary as the one "from whom seven demons had gone out." The implication is that the demons had been cast out by Jesus. Like so many people in her day and in ours, Mary's life was tortured by forces both within and without, forces that threatened to destroy her. The most vivid description of such a life in the New Testament is found in the story of Legion (Mark 5:1-20). Do you remember Mark's description of this tortured soul?

Outcast by the community in which he had lived, Legion lived in the cemetery. As far as his "neighbors" were concerned, he was as good as dead. They had tried to bind him with fetters and chains but to no avail. The forces that ravaged his soul also took their toll on his body as he went rampaging among the tombstones, bruising himself with the stones. Then one day Jesus came. He reached out to Legion in love and compassion. As a result, Legion was made whole again. When the townspeople came by they were amazed to see "the demonic sitting there, clothed and in his right mind" (Mark 5:14-15).

While we are given no detailed account of Mary's encounter with Jesus, the circumstances must have been essentially the same. Here was a woman who came to be known by all who encountered her as the woman with the demons. Like Legion she had probably become an outcast from her own community and had come to expect the same kind of treatment from everyone she met—scorn, ridicule, rebuke, rebuff. Then one day Jesus came. Rather than rebuff, he reached out to her in love. Rather than rebuke, he spoke of reconciliation, the reconciling of her life to the pattern of God's creative purpose for her life. Now she would be known, not as the woman with the seven demons, but as the woman "from whom seven demons had gone out." Mary was a new person, a new creation in Christ. It is not surprising that Mary became one of those who "followed" Jesus and "served" him.

In 2 Corinthians 5:17ff, the apostle Paul sets forth the heart of the gospel. He reminds us that "if anyone is in Christ, there is a new creation; everything old has passed away; see, everything has become new." So it was for Mary Magdalene. Then Paul reminds us that this new life is possible for all who have met this Christ, because "in Christ God was reconciling the world to himself." Mary had experienced this reconciliation, this re-creation in Jesus Christ. She stands for all time as an illustration of the transforming power of God's reconciling love as it has been made manifest to us in Christ Jesus.

Mary went on to become a minister of that reconciling love. She became one of those involved in what Paul describes in 2 Corinthians as "the ministry of reconciliation." Reconciliation occurs when we are willing to serve those around us. Luke tells us that Mary was characterized by a willingness to serve. She served her Lord to be sure, but she was also willing to serve her fellow disciples. Here we can learn a great deal from Mary. Too often we are all too anxious to serve Jesus, but all too unwilling to serve those around us. Conflict is inevitable when such an attitude prevails, even in the community of faith and love. We have seen it all too often. It is the result of an unwillingness to serve. Mary was willing to serve. Having been reconciled, she was ready to be a minister of reconciliation.

Faithful Come What May
Reflection Texts
John 19:25; 20:1-10

While each of the four Gospels highlights the role of the women who had followed Jesus from Galilee in the events surrounding the resurrection, Mary Magdalene is clearly the chief character in John's account. According to John 19:25, she was "standing by the cross" with Mary the mother of Jesus, her sister, and Mary the wife of Clopas. In Matthew 27:59-61, she was there when Joseph of Arimathea "took the body and wrapped it in a clean linen cloth and laid it in his own new tomb, which he had hewn in the rock." When he "rolled a great stone to the door of the tomb and went away," she was "sitting opposite the tomb."

Like many of the others, Mary must have been bewildered by the events that had transpired during the course of the past twenty-four hours. Bewildered, yes . . . but there was no going back on her commitment to her Lord. There is no hint of betrayal here—no skirting about in the shadows for fear of being seen, no fleeing the scene for fear of being identified with Jesus. Mary was openly unashamed of her loyalty to Jesus. One cannot help but think of Jesus' words on another occasion: "Everyone therefore who acknowledges me before others, I also will acknowledge before my Father in heaven" (Matt 10:32). Mary made her confession and stood by it even if it meant standing by a cross and sitting before a tomb!

Where were the Twelve during the long, seemingly endless, dark hours on that most dismal of days? We have no evidence of their presence at Calvary, no record of their attendance at the tomb. Where was Peter, the one who not more than twenty-four hours earlier had openly declared, "Even though all become deserters, I will not. . . . Even though I must die with you, I will not deny you" (Mark 14:29-31)? No such speeches are attributed to Mary—no brash words of bravado falling from her lips. All we get from Mary is the testimony of a follower who is faithful come what may!

Tried and true through the most demanding test of all, such faithfulness is expected of Jesus' disciples. The disciple of Jesus is called to journey with Jesus all the way to the cross and, if necessary, even to the tomb. Mary was there. When he took upon himself the crushing weight of human sin, Mary was there. She was faithful to stand with Jesus through it all.

The other disciples were nowhere to be found when the dark despair of death loomed across the sky, and the cross marked the horizon. We understand why. In our most honest moments, we, too, are wont to flee. "Give us the glory, but don't give us the cross!" If we take Jesus at his word, however, we must journey with him to dark Calvary and stand there with Mary. "If any want to become my followers, let them deny themselves and take up their cross and follow me" (Mark 8:34). Mary had heard that call. She was there, faithful to the end.

"Apostle to the Apostles"
Reflection Text
John 20:11-18

In all of the Gospels, the story is the same. When the Sabbath was over and the first day of the week came, Mary Magdalene led the women to the tomb. According to John's account, she found that the stone had been rolled away from the door of the tomb. Startled, she ran and found Peter and the beloved disciple and told them. They went to the tomb and discovered the tomb was empty as Mary had reported. When they left, she remained outside the tomb weeping. Her tears were to become the prism for the most incredible of sights, as suddenly the risen Christ appeared and spoke to her. At first she did not recognize him. Is it any wonder? Who among us would have expected to see

Jesus, the same Jesus we had seen brutally crucified, whose burial we had witnessed with our own eyes? Then he called her name, "Mary," and suddenly she knew it was him.

According to John, Mary recognized Jesus when he called her name. This fact had great theological significance for the Gospel writer. Turn back to John 10 and read verses 1-8. In these verses Jesus sets out in detail the nature of his relationship to his disciples using the analogy of a shepherd and his sheep. Notice verses 3 and 4. The sheep hear the shepherd's voice. In fact, "he calls his own sheep by name and leads them out. . . . he goes ahead of them, and the sheep follow him because they know his voice." Jesus is the great shepherd of the sheep. The sheep are his disciples. He calls his disciples by name. "Mary," he said to her, and she knew his voice as any genuine disciple would, for, as he said in verse 14, "I am the good shepherd; I know my own and my own know me." Finally, notice the words of John in 13:1:

> Now before the festival of the Passover, Jesus knew that his hour had come to depart from this world and go to the Father. Having loved his own who were in the world, he loved them to the end.

Who are "his own"? For John "his own" are persons such as Mary Magdalene who "know his voice" and "follow him," those who, like Mary, hear him call their name.

The rewards of Mary's faithfulness are clearly set before us. She received her commission from Jesus himself—the commission to announce the greatest news that the world has ever heard, the privilege of being the first to say "I have seen the Lord." Not only was Mary charged to announce the truth of the resurrection, also she would announce its significance. She would tell the others that the work of salvation had been completed. Jesus told her: "Go to my brothers, and say to them, I am ascending to my Father and your Father, to my God and your God" (20:17). On the cross he had said, "It is finished" (19:30).

Now they could be sure that it was so. Now the way to fellowship with God was open for all. Now the Lamb of God had taken away the sin of the world (John 1:29). Now "he has appeared once for all at the end of the age to remove sin by the sacrifice of himself" (Heb 9:26). To all who receive him, who believe in his name, he gives the power to become the children of God (John 1:12). His work complete, he has ascended to the one who is our Father and our God. This is the meaning of the resurrection. This is the meaning of "the miracle of Easter morning." This is the news that Mary was chosen to be the first to announce and that disciples have been called to announce ever since.

According to a tradition about Mary that dates back at least as far as the ninth century, Mary was known as "the apostle to the apostles." To her the apostolic message was first delivered. Peter and the beloved disciple left the tomb with nothing to announce but the mystery of a missing body. Mary brought the message, the "Good News" that the "missing body" was, in fact, a living Lord. In that sense, at least, the claim of the ancient tradition is true. Mary was "the apostle to the apostles." In her faithfulness to her Lord, she stands as a model for every generation of what it means to journey with Jesus.

Paul

Biblical Texts
Acts 9:1-22; 11:19-22; 13–28;
Galatians 1:11–2:16; Philippians 3:4-6

While we may know very little about some of the twelve apostles, the New Testament tells us a great deal about the disciple of Jesus who is sometimes referred to as "the thirteenth apostle." Not only does the book of Acts provide us with a record of the most important part of his life, but the New Testament also contains a collection of his letters. Here was a man whose impact on Christian history is second only to that of Jesus himself. Briefly let us review some of the significant details of Paul's life and ministry.

We first meet Paul in the book of Acts as Saul, the Jewish name he used until some time after his conversion. According to his own testimony, he was born the son of Hebrew parents (Phil 3:5) in the city of Tarsus, the capital of Cilicia that he justifiably referred to as "no mean city." Tarsus was a significant city situated on a rich plain, protected from cold winds by the lofty Taurus mountains to the north. Two great trade routes passed through Tarsus, one from the Euphrates valley and the other from Egypt via Palestine and Syria. From Tarsus they proceeded west.

In a very real sense, therefore, Tarsus was a meeting place of East and West, through which commercial and military expeditions had passed for centuries. It was also a great university city that attracted teachers and students from all over the Mediterranean world. Here Paul would learn the Greek language and culture that would enable him to preach all over the world. From his father he inherited the privilege of Roman citizenship. Like every Jewish boy, he learned a trade—in his case tentmaking, a skill that would serve him well in later years as he worked to support himself during many of his missionary travels.

Paul's father was a Pharisee, and Paul was no doubt brought up according to the strict Pharisaic understanding of the Jewish faith. In his early teens Saul probably set sail for Jerusalem where he continued his religious training with the great Pharisaic teacher Gamaliel. So highly was Gamaliel regarded by the Jews, it is said that with his death, reverence for the law ceased and purity and abstinence died away! Paul distinguished himself as a student who, according to his own testimony in Galatians 1:14, "advanced in Judaism beyond many among my people of the same age, for I was more zealous for the traditions of my ancestors." He seemed destined for a brilliant career as a distinguished rabbi.

Saul first appears in the New Testament as a persecutor of the church. According to Acts 7:5ff, he was present at the stoning of Stephen where "the witnesses laid their coats at the feet of a young man named Saul." As a result of Stephen's martyrdom, there arose a bitter persecution of Christians in Jerusalem. Many Christians were driven out of the city, with some apparently going to Damascus. We next meet Saul on the road to Damascus on his way to persecute the Christians there.

This was a very natural course of action for the Pharisee Saul. In his mind, Jesus could not possibly be the Messiah for several reasons. First, Jesus had violated the Law, at least, the oral law (what the Gospels refer to as the "traditions of the elders"). Surely anyone who violated the Law could not be the Messiah. Furthermore, Jesus' death seemed to confirm Saul's conclusion. He had, after all, died hanging on a tree, and the Old Testament made it clear that anyone who hangs on a tree was under God's curse (Deut 21:23). How could anyone under God's curse possibly be the Messiah? Thus, Saul set out to put a stop to the heresy of the Christians who proclaimed Jesus to be the Messiah.

On the road to Damascus, however, Saul was "arrested by Christ Jesus" (Phil 3:12). There he was confronted by Jesus Christ and forced to come to grips with the incredible reality that Jesus was alive, and if he was alive, then he must be the Messiah. Only God could raise someone from the dead, and if God had raised Jesus, this resurrection must be seen as God's vindication of all that Jesus had said and done. Thus, the cross itself, which had been for Saul the persecutor the sign of God's curse, became for Paul the place of revelation—the revelation of God's sacrificial love for sinful humanity.

Paul was received into the Christian fellowship in Damascus. What followed is not quite clear, but a careful study of information found in Acts 9 and Galatians 1 suggests that he first went into Arabia, then returned to Damascus where he began to proclaim Jesus as Messiah (Acts 9:22). Eventually he was forced to flee from Damascus for his own safety. His friends were forced to smuggle him over the city walls in a basket (v. 24; 2 Cor 11:32ff). Thus, about three years after his conversion, he went to Jerusalem (v. 26; Gal 1:18-24). Then he went back to his native city of Tarsus where he ministered for about ten years (Acts 9:30).

He reappeared in the city of Antioch in Syria when Barnabas, who had been sent to Antioch by the Jerusalem church, brought in Paul to assist him (Acts 11:22). Paul ministered alongside Barnabas until the two of them were sent out by the church in Antioch on what is sometimes referred to as the first missionary journey narrated in Acts 13–14. Paul's second mission is described in Acts 15:36–18:22, and a third is narrated in Acts 18:23–21:17. Beginning in Acts 21:18, Luke narrates Paul's journey to Rome after being arrested in Jerusalem at the conclusion of the third mission.

The book of Acts ends with Paul under house arrest in Rome. What happened to him after this is uncertain. One tradition declares that he was subsequently tried and acquitted, and that he continued his missionary work traveling as far as Spain before being rearrested and put to death. More than likely, at the end of the two years of house arrest mentioned in Acts 28:30, he was put to death in the Neronian persecution.

The only physical description we have of Paul comes from the apocryphal *Acts of Paul and Thecla,* which describes him as

> bald-headed, bow-legged, strongly built, a man small in size, with meeting eyebrows, with a rather large nose. . . . at times he looked like a man, and at times he had the face of angel.[1]

Whether this description is genuine or not, we cannot know, but we do know that our debt to Paul is greater than we can ever repay. Indeed,

> No man ever packed more achievement—more thinking and doing and suffering—into his earthly span. . . . beside the achievements of Paul of Tarsus the work of Alexander the Great or of Napoleon "pales into insignificance." Paul the tentmaker from Tarsus, pupil of Gamaliel, *civis Romanus,* apostle to the Gentiles, first of Christian mystics, most dynamic of Christian missionaries, supreme servant and interpreter of Christ, the most illustrious name in the roll-call of the saints.[2]

The book of Acts records many incidents that demonstrate the dynamic impact that Paul had on his world. Do you remember what happened when he went to the Greek city of Thessalonica? He and those with him proclaimed the gospel with such dynamism and power that they created quite a stir. As a result of the impact of Paul's ministry, Christians were brought before the city authorities. Do you remember the charge that was brought against them? It is recorded in Acts 17:6: "These people who have been turning the world upside down have come here also." What characteristic about Paul enabled him to live his life in such a way that wherever he went he literally turned the world upside down? What was the secret of his dynamic discipleship? Let us look together at three of the keys to dynamic discipleship that are reflected in Paul's life.

To Live Is Christ
Reflection Text
Philippians 1:21

In his letter to the Philippian church, Paul reminds his readers that he had been "arrested" by Jesus Christ (Phil 3:12). He was referring, of course, to that fateful day on the road to Damascus road when he was confronted by the risen Christ. He was on his way from Jerusalem to Damascus, his briefcase bulging with warrants for the arrest of the followers of the crucified Jesus. Then it happened. On the Damascus road Paul met the risen Christ, and in a moment—in the twinkling of an eye—his whole world was turned upside down!

If the crucified Jesus was alive, it could only mean one thing: God had raised him from the dead. If God had raised him from the dead, Jesus was indeed the Messiah. If Jesus was the Messiah, then as far as Paul was concerned, that could only mean one thing: he must spend the rest of his life serving this Christ—which is exactly what he did. He turned his back on what would no doubt have been a brilliant career as a rabbi. He turned his back on the accolades and applause of family and friends and spent the rest of his life whistle-stopping his way around the Roman Empire preaching to anyone who would hear the Good News about Jesus Christ. For Paul, to live *was* Christ!

Paul's story is an incredible story. It is the story of an exceptional commitment—exceptional in the sense that it is seldom seen. But . . . is the kind of commitment manifested in Paul's life meant to be the exception? Not in Paul's mind, not for one moment. Paul challenged the Philippians to imitate him and others who followed Christ. As far as Paul was concerned, this kind of commitment was not to be the exception but the rule for disciples of Jesus. Every Christian should be prepared to join him and declare "For me, to live is Christ! He is priority number one in my life. He is the center of my universe. Everything I am, everything I have, everything I ever hope to be revolves around him. For me to live *is* Christ!"

In his book *A Soldier's Story of the Allied Campaigns from Tunis to the Elbe,* General Omar Bradley tells of the brilliant though brief combat career of Colonel Paddy Flint. Though somewhat eccentric, Flint was known for his boldness and indomitable spirit. Bradley tells how in an effort to inspire his troops Flint had painted the following letters on the side of his helmet: AAA-0. These letters were intended to communicate to his troops that he was committed to accomplishing his mission no matter what the cost.[3] The AAA-0 stood for "Anything, Anywhere, Anytime bar Nothing!"

The apostle Paul wore no helmet on which to paint those letters, but persons who knew him must have understood that such was the nature of his commitment to Christ. It was an "anything, anywhere, anytime bar nothing" kind of commitment. That is the implication of the words, "For to me, to live *is* Christ."

To Share the Gospel
Reflection Text
Romans 1:16

The nature of Paul's commitment was clearly manifested in his commitment to sharing the gospel with others. Nowhere is this commitment more clearly expressed than in Roman 1:16: "For I am not ashamed of the gospel; it is the power of God for salvation to everyone who has faith." In Romans 1–8 Paul sets out his understanding of the nature of this gospel. It consists of a clear recognition of and statement of the human predicament that Paul summarizes in Romans 3:23: "All have sinned and fall short of the glory of God." The fact is: no one is righteous, no not one. Humanity is involved in an insurrection against God—a rebellion against God's lordship. It is a revolt in which we are all involved, and the end result of this rebellion is our own destruction and death, for "the wages of sin is death."

This fundamental understanding of the human condition makes the gospel such "good news," for the gospel not only recognizes the human predicament but also announces the divine solution. The gospel proclaims the incredible news that God has acted to remedy the tragic situation, for "while we were still sinners Christ died for us" (Rom 5:8). In 2 Corinthians 5:18-19, Paul puts it another way: "In Christ God was reconciling the world to himself, not counting their trespasses

against them." The good news is that, while we were dead in our trespasses and sins, God has taken the initiative to reconcile us to God's
self to forgive our sins that we might live in fellowship with God.
Thanks be to God! This message can make an eternal difference in the
life of every man, woman, girl, and boy. Paul set out to share this message with everyone he met.

The depth of Paul's commitment to sharing this message is clearly
illustrated in the story of his ministry in the city of Lystra (Acts 14:19-
20). Paul entered the city where he began to share the gospel with all
who would listen. As time passed, some persons who were disturbed
by the message that Paul preached and who were unwilling to accept
the gospel began to stone him. Finally, he was beaten down by stones
until he lay unconscious on the side of the road as if he were dead. His
opponents left, confident that they had silenced him once and for all,
while those who were sympathetic to his message gathered around
him. When Paul began to regain consciousness, those who had gathered around began to encourage him to move on to another town. It
seemed the logical thing to do. Do you remember what Paul did? He
got up from the roadside and marched back into Lystra where he
shared the gospel once again! For Paul, you see, sharing the gospel
with others was more important than life itself! This was the nature of
his commitment to witness for Christ.

Is such a commitment to witnessing exceptional? Once again, it
may be exceptional in the sense that those who demonstrate such a
commitment are the exception, but should it be the exception or the
rule? Do you remember Jesus' last words to his disciples? "You will be
my witnesses" (Acts 1:8). Did he say, "Occasionally will you be my
witnesses" or "If it is not too inconvenient, will you be my witnesses?"
No! Jesus said, "You *will* be my witnesses." Jesus assumed that his disciples would be his witnesses! There can be no question but that the
apostle Paul took Jesus seriously. The question is, do we?

To Live for the Glory of God
Reflection Text
1 Corinthians 10:31

In his letter to the troubled church in Corinth, Paul suggests another of
the keys to dynamic discipleship. Listen to his exhortation in 1
Corinthians 10:31: "So, whether you eat or drink, or whatever you do,
do everything to the glory of God." This principle governed Paul's
behavior. It was his guide as he took his Christian commitment from

the comfortable pew to the busy streets of the Roman world. It was based on Paul's conviction that he served a risen and living Christ, the Christ he had met on the Damascus road.

Like Paul we profess our faith in the resurrection of Jesus. On Easter Sunday we announce to the world our belief that Jesus is not dead but a living Lord. Indeed, we worship on Sunday as a celebration of our belief that Jesus rose on the first day of the week. We sing, "He lives, he lives, Christ Jesus lives today. He walks with me and talks with me along life's narrow way." Indeed, like Paul we claim to believe in the resurrected Christ, but do we live as if Jesus really lives? Do we live our lives as if Jesus is alive and present with us in every situation and circumstance? Is the way we live our lives each day a direct reflection of the depth of our belief in the resurrection? Do we live as if Jesus lives? When we do, then we will do whatever we do to the glory of God!

What characteristic about Paul enabled him to live his life in such a way that wherever he went he literally turned the world upside down? What was the secret of his dynamic discipleship? Perhaps the answer is all too clear. Living in light of the resurrection, Paul did whatever he did to the glory of God. He gave his life to share the gospel regardless of the price he had to pay. His was an "anything, anywhere, anytime bar nothing" commitment to Christ's lordship, for to Paul to live was Christ. When this is the nature of our commitment too, when we are serious about our journey with Jesus as were the first disciples, then once again we may hear people begin to say, "These people who have turned the world upside down have come here also."

Notes

[1]*Acts of Paul and Thecla,* 2.

[2]A. M. Hunter, *Introducing the New Testament,* 3rd rev. ed. (Philadelphia: Westminster, 1972) 91.

[3]Omar Bradley, *A Soldier's Story of the Allied Campaign from Tunis to the Elbe* (London: Eyre and Spottiswoode, 1951) 153.